F. Shackelford

The Great Jew and the Great German

F. Shackelford

The Great Jew and the Great German

ISBN/EAN: 9783337148393

Printed in Europe, USA, Canada, Australia, Japan

Cover: Foto ©ninafisch / pixelio.de

More available books at **www.hansebooks.com**

THE GREAT JEW

AND

THE GREAT GERMAN

OR

FROM PAUL TO LUTHER

A HISTORICAL STUDY

BY

F. H. SHACKELFORD

NEW YORK
WILLIAM BEVERLEY HARISON
No. 59 FIFTH AVENUE

All rights reserved

PREFACE.

THE long reach of time, crowded with momentous events and movements, which stretches between the Great Jew and the Great German, renders it impossible for men and women who live amidst the press and stress of business, and the absorbing and daily recurring cares of life, to acquire a clear and connected knowledge of the important links in the long and knotted chain of events, which brought Western Europe from barbarism, and made of her, and through her of America, leaders in the van-guard of human progression. Therefore this little book goes forth as a convenient treasure-house of knowledge, in which may be found consecutively traced, the founding, and the formative period of Christianity, its lines of religious and civil development, and its deformative period, together with its reformative period—The Reformation.

The religion of all people, lies at the root of their civilization and subsequent culture; and the fact that Europe and America lead the nations of the world, is to be mainly attributed to the divine vitality of Christianity, which notwithstanding the manifold degeneracies and backslidings of Christendom, has still guided Christian nations onward to a purer and higher humanity.

Under the blessing of God, may this little book prove helpful to thousands of readers.

BALTIMORE, MD. THE AUTHOR.

TABLE OF CONTENTS.

PART I.

CHAPTER I.
THE APOSTOLIC CALL—THE TRIBAL NUMBER, BROKEN THROUGH JUDAS ISCARIOT, RESTORED THROUGH THE ELECTION OF MATTHIAS.

CHAPTER II.
SAUL OF TARSUS—A GLIMPSE OF HIS EARLY LIFE—HIS CONVERSION.

CHAPTER III.
SAUL'S RETIREMENT AND PREPARATION FOR HIS GREAT LIFE-WORK—PUBLIC MINISTRY—CHANGE OF NAME.

CHAPTER IV.
FIRST CHURCH COUNCIL, HELD IN JERUSALEM, ST. JAMES PRESIDING—DECREE OF THE COUNCIL—LABORS AND PERILS OF ST. PAUL.

CHAPTER V.
THE SCHOLARLY PAUL IN CLASSIC ATHENS—THE AREOPAGUS—CONTINUED LABORS—TUMULT IN EPHESUS.

CHAPTER VI.
ENVY AND JEALOUSY PROMPT FALSE CHARGES AGAINST THE GREAT APOSTLE—HE GOES TO JERUSALEM TO SET HIMSELF RIGHT WITH THE MOTHER CHURCH—BROUGHT BEFORE ROMAN GOVERNORS—VOYAGE TO ROME—IMPRISONMENT, TRIAL, ACQUITTAL.

CHAPTER VII.
PERSONAL APPEARANCE OF ST. PAUL—MEDALLION FIND AT HERCULANEUM.

CHAPTER VIII.

THE EPISTLES OF ST. PAUL, THE FOUNTAIN HEAD OF CHRISTIAN PHILOSOPHY—CHRONOLOGICAL ARRANGEMENT.

PART II.

CHAPTER IX.

THE PRIMITIVE CHURCH, ONE HOUSEHOLD IN THE FAITH—DIRE PERSECUTIONS UNDER PAGAN EMPERORS—CONSTANTINE—OUTWARD PEACE TO THE CHURCH—INWARD DISCORD AND BITTERNESS—THE FAMOUS COUNCIL OF NICÆ.

CHAPTER X.

SEAT OF EMPIRE REMOVED TO CONSTANTINOPLE—THE BISHOP OF ROME ACQUIRES GREATER INFLUENCE IN AFFAIRS OF STATE—GROWING DESIRE IN THE WESTERN CHURCH FOR A DEFINITE CONSTITUTION.

CHAPTER XI.

THE EARLY MONKS, THEIR INDUSTRY AND FRUGALITY—MONASTIC AND CATHEDRAL SCHOOLS—MONASTERIES GROW RICH, IDLENESS AND DEGENERACY ENSUE—EFFORTS FOR REFORM—CHRISTIANITY, THE MAINSPRING OF THE RELIGIOUS AND CIVIL SUPERIORITY OF WESTERN EUROPE—THE VENERABLE BEDE—CHARLEMAGNE.

CHAPTER XII.

ERIGENA SCOTUS—HIS EXPOSITION OF CHRISTIAN PHILOSOPHY—ALFRED THE GREAT.

CHAPTER XIII.

THE CRUSADES—PETER THE HERMIT—BERNARD OF CLAIRVAUX—GROWTH OF PAPAL POWER—MENDICANT MONKS—COURT OF THE INQUISITION ESTABLISHED.

CHAPTER XIV.

PAPAL COURT REMOVED TO AVIGNON—WARS BETWEEN PAPAL FACTIONS—SPIRITUAL DEGENERACY—CIVIL PROSPECTS BRIGHTEN—HANSEATIC LEAGUE—SPANISH ARABS—ROGER BACON.

CHAPTER XV.

THE INTELLECTUAL HORIZON BRIGHTENS IN ITALY, FRANCE, ENGLAND AND GERMANY—WYCLIFFE TRANSLATES THE BIBLE INTO ENGLISH.

PART III.

CHAPTER XVI.

THE REVIVAL OF LEARNING—GREAT DISCOVERIES AND INVENTIONS—COPERNICUS—COLUMBUS—THE WORLD'S MASTER ART—PRINTING.

CHAPTER XVII.

SIR THOMAS MORE—ERASMUS—TURBULENCE IN ROME—POPE NICHOLAS V.—WICKEDNESS INCARNATE—SIXTUS IV—INNOCENT VIII.—ALEXANDER VI.

CHAPTER XVIII.

ROBERT GREATHEAD, BISHOP OF LINCOLN, THE MORNING STAR OF THE REFORMATION—JOHN WYCLIFFE, HIS SON IN THE GOSPEL—DR. MARTIN LUTHER—POPE LEO X.—CONFERENCE AT AUGSBURG.

CHAPTER XIX.

THE DIET OF WORMS—THE ELECTOR, FREDERIC THE WISE—THE KNIGHT GEORGE, PRISONER IN THE FORTRESS OF WARTBURG.

CHAPTER XX.

LUTHER TRANSLATES THE BIBLE INTO GERMAN—CHARACTERISTICS OF LUTHER—ULRICH ZWINGLI.

CHAPTER XXI.

ABBEY OF EINSIEDLEN—ZWINGLI CALLED TO ZURICH—PUBLIC CONFERENCES IN ZURICH.

CHAPTER XXII.

THE SWISS REFORMATION, AN AUTHORIZED NATIONAL MOVEMENT—THE WORSHIP OF IMAGES CONDEMNED, THE MASS ABOLISHED—MONASTERIES SUPPRESSED—YOUNG AND ROBUST MONKS MUST LEARN TRADES.

CHAPTER XXIII.

UNION OF REFORMED CANTONS—CIVIL WAR—LAMENTED DEATH OF ULRICH ZWINGLI—JOHN CALVIN, HEAD OF THE REFORMED CHURCH OF GENEVA.

CHAPTER XXIV.

THEOCRATIC GOVERNMENT ESTABLISHED IN GENEVA—CIVIL TROUBLES—CALVIN'S PERSONAL COURAGE—SERVETUS.

CHAPTER XXV.

REFORM MOVEMENT IN FRANCE—PRINCE OF CONDE, ADMIRAL COLIGNY, THE QUEEN OF NAVARRE, AND DUCHESS OF FERRARA, LEADERS IN THE MOVEMENT—HENRY OF NAVARRE, CROWNED HENRY IV. OF FRANCE, ISSUES THE EDICT OF NANTES—REFORMERS PROTECTED—FATAL REVOCATION OF THE EDICT OF NANTES, BY LOUIS XIV.

CHAPTER XXVI.

ENGLISH REFORMATION—CARDINAL WOLSEY—SUPPRESSION OF THE MONASTERIES—ARCHBISHOP CRANMER—CHURCH CONVOCATIONS—SEPARATION OF THE CHURCH OF ENGLAND FROM THE CHURCH OF ROME—BISHOP'S BIBLE—TYNDALE'S NEW TESTAMENT, IN ENGLISH.

CHAPTER XXVII.

DEATH OF HENRY VIII.—THE KINGLY BOY, EDWARD VI.—BOOK OF COMMON PRAYER—BLOODY MARY.

CHAPTER XXVIII.

QUEEN ELIZABETH—LIBERTY OF RELIGIOUS BELIEF—PAPAL PLOT TO ASSASSINATE THE QUEEN, CROWN MARY OF SCOTLAND, AND PLACE ENGLAND AT THE FEET OF THE POPE—CARDINAL OF LORRAINE—DUKE OF GUISE.

PART IV.

CHAPTER XXIX.

THE IMPORTANT REPUBLIC OF FLORENCE—DANTE—COSMO DI MEDICI—A PIONEER OF THE RENAISSANCE, AND CHIEF RULER—FATHER OF HIS COUNTRY.

CHAPTER XXX.
POPE SIXTUS IV.—PLOT AGAINST THE DI MEDICI, HATCHED IN ROME.

CHAPTER XXXI.
BULL OF EXCOMMUNICATION HURLED AGAINST FLORENCE—"LORENZO THE MAGNIFICENT," WISE AND LIBERAL RULER, LEADER IN THE REVIVAL OF LEARNING, FRIEND AND PATRON OF ARTISTS AND MEN OF LETTERS—SAVONAROLA, PROPHET-PRIEST, PRIOR OF SAN MARCO.

CHAPTER XXXII.
SAVONAROLA, SUPREME RULER OF FLORENCE—HIS AUSTERITIES BRING HIM IN CONFLICT WITH POPE AND PEOPLE—HIS ARREST—SUFFERINGS—TERRIBLE DEATH.

CHAPTER XXXIII.
SAVONAROLA, A HARBINGER OF THE REFORMATION, THOUGH NARROW AND MONKISH IN HIS REFORMS—HIS CLAIM TO THE PROPHETIC OFFICE.

CHAPTER XXXIV.
MICHAEL ANGELO—THE ART KING—HIS GREAT WORKS—DEATH AND FUNERAL HONORS.

CHAPTER XXXV.
MACHIAVELLI—HISTORIAN OF FLORENCE—FATHER OF MODERN HISTORY.

INTRODUCTION.

The epistles of St. Paul have ever been a favorite theme with Christian writers, and every year adds to the already voluminous literature on this subject, which is mainly polemical. And the life of St. Paul has been written out as fully as the materials would allow by many able writers. But the reader of this little volume will find in it the salient points of the great man's character and career succinctly drawn and harmoniously grouped. The general reader needs nothing more to exhibit to him "the chiefest of the apostles" in all his sublime moral and mental grandeur.

Throughout the work, extending from the first to the sixteenth century, the historic continuity is clearly preserved, and the inherent power of Christianity to elevate humanity to higher planes of life, notwithstanding all the persecution, enmity and unbelief of ungodly men, without and within the church, is traced with the earnestness of strong conviction, and with a fervor of spirit which none but one familiar with the subject, both spiritually and intellectually, could exhibit.

Throughout the book the author never hesitates to express personal convictions pretty strongly, though full and impartial justice is done to every character and event which it was necessary to introduce. From the beginning to the end, evidence is everywhere displayed of large sympathies and discriminating judgment.

The brief parallel run between St. Paul and Luther is thoughtful and just; every student of history must discern many striking points of similarity in the character and career of the great Apostle and the illustrious Reformer.

Taken as a whole, this modest little volume is a goodly array of carefully culled fruit, of tempting variety and richness, and is invitingly set before us on a clean porcelain platter.

The book is specially adapted to Sunday-schools and to the majority of lay readers; its pages are not loaded down with references to learned authorities, by which the facts stated may be verified; instead, the author moves smoothly along the line of investigation, authenticating facts as they are stated, thereby saving the reader both the labor and the time necessary to hunt up authorities, had he the inclination to do so.

We heartily commend this little book to the general public. Its style is pure, simple and elegant, its historical correctness accords with the best authorities known to literature. And above all, we commend it for the intelligent apprehension of the nature and influence of the gospel of Christ, which pervades its pages.

J. G. MORRIS, D. D.

THE JEW AND THE GERMAN,

OR

FROM PAUL TO LUTHER.

PART I.

CHAPTER I.

THE TRIBAL NUMBER.

As the aroma of flowers lingers in the perfume-scented air long after the flowers have perished, even so does the influence of once deeply-rooted beliefs linger in human speech and usage long after the beliefs have perished. This may be clearly seen in the far-reaching influence of that very ancient and world-wide belief in *numbers,* or rather in the inherent power of certain numbers to affect for good or ill the destiny of man. In varying degrees this influence may be traced up the ascent of the ages from the remote past even unto this present time.

In sacred scripture, particularly in the books of the Old Bible, the frequent recurrence of the numbers seven, ten, twelve and forty, comes to the thoughtful reader as a voice from out the ages when the human race was young. And in the fullness of time, when the Blessed Master entered upon his public ministry,. he saw fit, in choosing his disciples, to honor Israel's tribal number. And those twelve chosen men enjoyed the inestimable privilege of daily and intimate association with Jesus. Day by day, for the space of three years, those twelve men listened to His gracious words of life,—and they witnessed His wonderful works. And most of them lived to see the middle wall of partition, which had shut off the Gentile from the privileges of the Jew, broken down through the faithful preaching of the gospel of Christ, the good tidings which abolished the law of commandments contained in ordinances, the good tidings of the common brotherhood of man, of the all-fatherhood of Him who is no respecter of persons. And in the gospel of Christ, they saw, as we may see, an index finger pointing beyond the Jordan of death to the unseen Kingdom of Heaven, the complement of the Kingdom of Heaven which is at hand.

The daily life of Jesus was a humble life, his habits were simple, his wants were few, and those few were easily supplied. Possibly the perfect content of Jesus with his lowly manner of life was such a bitter disappointment to the national ambition of Judas Iscariot that the loss of his belief in Jesus as the restorer of the throne of David, and consequently of all hope of personal aggrandizement, led him to betray his Master. An ancient tradition states that when Judas bargained with the chief priests it was with the understanding that Jesus should be restrained and silenced by arrest and imprisonment, but was not to be personally injured. Be that as it may, it is certain that the guilty man was unspeakably wretched when he learned the fatal result of his crime. Instead of merely arrest and detention by imprisonment, the Master was led in the cold night before bigoted Jewish judges; exposed to the senseless fury of a fickle mob, to the blind scorn of mockers, and to the awful sentence of crucifixion on Calvary. The miserable man could bear up no longer. St. Matthew says, "When he saw that he (the Master) was condemned, he repented himself." The wretched man went to the chief priests and casting down the thirty pieces of silver, and condemning himself as the betrayer of innocent blood, went forth in such agony of soul, that falling headlong, in his endeavor to hang himself, he burst asunder in the midst and all his bowels gushed out. Repentant, miserable Judas!

The place which Judas by transgression lost, fervent-minded, impulsive Peter sought to fill from among those who had companied with them all the time the Lord Jesus went in and out among them.

In the days of their bereavement the little church was wont to gather for prayer in an upper chamber in the city of Jerusalem. It was to one of these gatherings that Peter submitted his proposition. It was received with favor, and prayer was offered and lots were cast, and the lot fell upon Matthias, and he was numbered among the twelve. The tribal number, honored of the Master, was again complete; but no further mention is made of Matthias, though he may have been a faithful and efficient apostle of Christ; had it been otherwise, it would doubtless have been mentioned, for the sacred writers are not chary in speaking of the short-comings of their brethren; they tell their story simply and plainly.

CHAPTER II.

SAUL OF TARSUS.

OUTSIDE of the sacred number, and not until some three years later, is seen in the church the great light of the apostolic age. For him no lots were cast; he was called and sent forth by the risen Jesus, and he responded to his call with whole-hearted faith, a faith that to the end never faltered.

Saul of Tarsus, The Chosen Vessel, received his peril-fraught commission directly from the risen Saviour. And by his labors, instant in season and out of season, both among Jews and Gentiles, he lifted the church of Christ above a local faction, or segment of the Jewish church, and started her on her path of world-conquest, a path on which she has continued to move from that day to this, though the pathway has at times been devious, even retrograde, but in the main it has ever been upward, and the church of Christ has been gathering into her fold from among all the tribes and nations of men.

A memoir of the early life of Saul of Tarsus would be a valuable addition to biographical literature, but unfortunately the thick veil of oblivion hides away all reliable information on the subject. He was probably an only son, as a brother is nowhere mentioned; a sister and her son are mentioned. And it is equally probable, as his life from his youth up was spent in the great liberal school of Hillel, that his father was a man of wealth, as well as a Roman citizen. St. Paul's inherited right of Roman citizenship often stood him in good stead; and his lack of means of support compelling him to work at his trade of tent-making for his daily bread, rather than be chargeable to any, is an indication, if not a proof, that he had been disinherited. His father was no doubt keenly disappointed in the son whose learning and talents were already beginning to bear the fruit of high renown, when he suddenly turned his back upon the gathering honors of the world by identifying himself with the despised sect of the Nazarenes. That he had thereby lost all the gains of this world, is made clear in his letter to the Philippians; he writes, "What things were gain to me, these have I counted loss for Christ." And again, "I count all things to be loss for the excellency of the knowledge of Christ Jesus my Lord, for whom I suffered the loss of all things." *The loss of all things* necessarily includes not only his patrimony, but the high position he had attained among his people, and the yet higher reach that lay before him. But all these things, home, family ties, opulence, fame, and high worldly position, he counted but refuse, that he might gain Christ, not having the righteousness which is of the law, but that which is through faith in Christ, the righteousness which is of God by faith.

Jewish children were not received as responsible members of the great national church until after they had attained the age of twelve years; having reached the required age, the father was accounted in duty bound to have his children enrolled as responsible subjects of the Law. And as Saul lived in Jerusalem from his youth up, it is a legitimate conclusion that shortly after the promising boy had reached the lawful age, his father took him to Jerusalem, to be duly inducted into the church, and to place him in the famous school of Hillel, to be brought up at the feet of the wise Gamaliel—grandson of Hillel the founder, and his worthy successor.

The evidence in proof of the fact that St. Paul went to Jerusalem at an early age, and remained there through his youth, and up to early manhood, may be found in his words before Festus and Agrippa: "My manner of life from my youth up, which was among mine own nation, at Jerusalem, know all the Jews."

When the boy had grown into the young man, crowned with the honors of that famous liberal school, so wisely chosen by his father, he returned to his home at Tarsus, in the exulting strength of gifted and learned, young manhood, zealous for the honor of the Law, and for the glory of the God of his fathers.

Saul's return to Tarsus must have been previous to the entrance of Christ upon his public ministry, as the apostle speaks of having seen Jesus only in visions, therefore he could not have been living in Jerusalem during the three years of Christ's public ministry. Those three years were probably spent by the young man in Tarsus, partly in learning his craft of tent-making. All young Jews were required to learn a trade, the sons of the rich as well as the sons of the poor; a practical proof of Hebrew loyalty to their belief in the dignity as well as the necessity of labor. But in larger part he doubtless spent his precious time in laboring with fervent zeal, and vehement eloquence, to purge the church of the God of Israel from the defiling influence of Hellenizing teachers.

The growing fame of the young defender of the faith in Tarsus may have induced the Sanhedrim to offer to the young man a seat in their august court, and to take the necessary steps to carry out their offer. Tradition says that Saul of Tarsus was a member of the Sanhedrim. The Jewish law required that the members of the Sanhedrim should be elderly men and heads of families, but under the Herods, the law was loosely held; the high priesthood could be bought by any Levite who had sufficient money. Under such a state of affairs, it is not surprising that a man of distinguished ability, though young and unmarried, should be chosen a member of the Sanhedrim. But nothing is known particularly of Saul of Tarsus until he appears as the fierce persecutor of Christians. Not content with persecuting the Christians of Jerusalem, he sought from the Sanhedrim a commission to extend his persecuting fury even to a distant Syrian city.

The fierce persecuting spirit which took possession of the young man was foreign to his own nature, and in direct opposition to the liberal teaching of Gamaliel; it was the outward expression of intense inward agitation.

As an eloquent and over-zealous defender of the ancient faith, Saul may have had occasional disputations with preachers of the Christian faith, but most probably met no equal in the contest, until he met the gifted and intrepid Stephen.

The last great and fearless, but unfinished speech of Stephen, must have strongly moved the heart of the young Pharisee, and opened his spiritual eyes, to see as he had never seen before; that Abraham, Moses, and the ceremonial law led up to better things in Jesus; to see the hallowed past in its rightful relation of father to the present.

These new and disturbing thoughts and feelings wrought upon the young man until they drove him to a pitch of spiritual desperation, under the dread fear of his perfect orthodoxy being imperiled by the haunting power of Stephen's profound and fearless apology; this dread fear urged him on, with mad zeal, to root out a heresy which was knocking for entrance even at his own stout heart. But he could not silence the voice within; the conflict waxed sorer, until it was stilled by the voice of the Master, without the gate of Damascus, confirming the truth which Stephen had taught.

The persecutions of Saul in Jerusalem had been carried out as soon as resolved upon, but now, being duly commissioned by the Sanhedrim to seek out and bring bound to Jerusalem all Christians in the distant city of Damascus, the delay, occasioned by a long journey, comes between purpose and execution, giving opportunity for recollection and self-communion. No doubt the speech of Stephen came out from the recesses of his memory, and forced itself upon his attention; nor could he by the most adroit exercise of his fine logical power overthrow Stephen's conclusive line of argument, neither could he refuse to consider the holy heroism of the man, who, under the fearful torture of death by stoning, prayed for his murderers.

Such recollections must have intensified Saul's fierce struggle against a sense of self-condemnation, however much he might strive to fortify himself on the impregnable ground of duty to the God of his fathers. Great blows must have fallen on his heart, hurting more sorely than those of the goads on unruly oxen.

Saul was doubtless oblivious to the discomforts of his desert travel, unmindful of the ardent rays of the blazing Syrian sun; and from the nature of the case the journey must have been a silent one to Saul, for a mind oppressed and ill at ease is not a communicative mind.

As they near Damascus, city of surpassing beauty, behold! fearful lights begin to flash about the weary travellers, and suddenly, from out of heaven blazes a great light, which pales the noon-day sun; Saul and his companions fall prostrate with their faces to the earth; an awful, unintelligible sound stuns the ears of the men with Saul, but to his consciousness the awful sound came articulate and clear,—the voice of the Son of Man. But in that dread hour, Saul does not yield without question: "Who art thou, Lord?" The ear of his spirit is open, he hears in answer: "I am Jesus, whom thou persecutest."

Saul's companions arose from the earth and stood astounded; he too arose and opened his eyes, but saw nothing,—he was blind. The men with him led him by the hand into Damascus, and for three days he remained in his blindness, without meat or drink, in the house of Judas.

CHAPTER III.

Public Ministry, Change of Name.

Those three days were epoch-marking days, days which brought to birth The Chosen Vessel to bear the name of the Lord "before the Gentiles and Kings, and the Children of Israel."

In the book of the Acts of the Apostles, St. Luke records in graphic detail the incidents connected with the visit of Ananias to Saul, of Saul's recovery of sight, and of his baptism.

An entirely new direction was given to Saul's life through his conversion to Christianity. The bigoted pharisaism in which he had striven to excel his brethren was uprooted and cast out; his fervid zeal for the traditions of his fathers, gave place to an earnest desire to obtain a clearer apprehension of the great truths of the Gospel of Christ. To a mind like Saul's, a clearer and fuller knowledge of the faith he had embraced was a necessity, and would necessarily include a period of retirement from the bustle and business of life, and that such was the case, may be learned from his own words. He says, "I conferred not with flesh and blood, neither went I up to Jerusalem to them which were apostles before me, but I went away into Arabia." The context favors the conclusion that he remained in Arabia about three years; a period of solitary preparation for his great life work,—through meditation, prayer, and careful study of all the records he could obtain of the life and teachings of Jesus Christ. That such records were written very early in the history of the church is evident from the opening chapter of the Gospel according to St. Luke; and tradition tells that St.

Bartholomew gave to the church in India an original Hebrew document, containing the discourses of Christ, written out by St. Matthew.

In that age, wherever Greek culture had gained a footing, historical composition was an important art, and generally practiced. And as Ananias was a prominent man in the Damascan church, he would most probably be in possession of those precious documents on which the future development of the new doctrine must mainly depend, and he would be happy to lend them to the young man, whom he knew to be a Chosen Vessel of the Lord

After his long sojourn in Arabia, Saul returned to Damascus, and at once entered the field of the Christian ministry, though he was desirous to go up to Jerusalem and meet Peter and other fathers in the Christian faith. In writing to the church in Galatia, after referring to his calling to preach Christ among the Gentiles, to his sojourn in Arabia, and to his return to Damascus, he adds, "I went up to Jerusalem to become acquainted with Cephas"—Peter. On that visit he seems to have met only Peter and James.

Saul may have felt specially drawn at that time to St. Peter from having learned that, like himself, Peter had been sent to declare the gospel to the Gentiles, and had been divinely taught to call nothing common or unclean which God had cleansed.

When Saul began his public ministry in Damascus by expounding and defending the faith which he had so bitterly persecuted, the Jews in Damascus were astounded. The story of his persecuting commission, and of his blindness, had been current news three years before, and hearing nothing further from him, they regarded him as dead to the active affairs of life. His restoration to sight was a matter amongst Christians, and they had been taught through persecution to keep their own counsel. The Jews were probably of the opinion that Saul's sudden stroke of blindness had alone prevented his carrying out the commission of the Sanhedrim, and hence they were astounded at his reappearance with restored sight, and preaching the gospel he had persecuted unto the death. But their amazement soon turned into murderous wrath, and they took measures to kill him; but those measures were made known to the brethren, and being forewarned they were forearmed. His enemies, suspecting that he would try to make his escape from the city, watched the gates by day and by night to seize him, should he attempt to pass out. But friends, too, were on the alert, and some of them must have lived in a house built in or upon the wall, for while his enemies, with murder in their hearts, were watching by night at the gates of the city, they, under the sheltering wing of that same night, let him down in a basket through a window in the wall.

When Saul assayed to join the company of disciples in Jerusalem, they shrank from him. It seemed a thing incredible that the fierce persecutor, whose very name was a terror to the people into whose homes he had entered to hale men and women to prison because they were followers of Jesus, should verily have become a fellow-disciple. But Barnabas had knowledge of the wonderful change which had been wrought in Saul, and he bore witness to the powerful teachings of Saul at Damascus in the name of Jesus. Then the disciples gladly received him into their fellowship, and he preached boldly in the name of Jesus, which again brought Jewish wrath on his devoted head, and they sought to slay him. Again he was saved by the brethren, who brought him down to Cesarea and sent him forth to Tarsus.

Some time after, Barnabas sought him in Tarsus, and Saul returned with him to Antioch, and for the space of a year they labored in the church at Antioch, teaching much people. In the city of Antioch the term Christian was first applied to the disciples of Christ.

The Antiochian church, learning from the prophet Agabus and from others of the pressure of poverty on the churches of Judea, determined to send relief to the suffering brethren who dwelt in Judea. Every man of the church contributed according to his ability, and the amount raised was sent to the elders by Barnabas and Saul. When they had finished their ministrations they returned from Jerusalem, taking with them John, whose surname was Mark.

In the church at Antioch were certain prophets and teachers, among them Manaen, the foster brother of Herod the tetrarch. As these men ministered to the Lord and fasted, the Holy Spirit spoke to them: "Separate me Barnabas and Saul for the work whereunto I have called them." When they had fasted and prayed they laid their hands on Barnabas and Saul, and thereafter sent them away.

Thenceforth, in minute detail, St. Luke, in the Acts of the Apostles, records the carrying of the Gospel to the heathen, and Saul becomes the central figure, around whom a halo of glory gathers, growing brighter as the ages move on.

After he enters upon his peculiar mission, of apostle to the Gentiles, we hear no more of Saul, but of Paul, which may have been a Gentile form of his Hebrew name; or, according to some traditions, the combined name, Saul Paulus, was given at his birth. Those traditions possess a certain force of evidence, it being most probable that a Hebrew-Roman name would be given to the son of a Hebrew-Roman citizen; and from remote antiquity it was not unusual to combine Hebrew and Gentile names, and after the Roman occupation of Judea, it was of common occurrence, Herod Agrippa, Simon Peter, and so on.

CHAPTER IV.

First Church Council.

DID our limits permit, it would be a labor of love to gather up the salient points on the first missionary journey of St. Paul to the Gentiles, and record some of his glowing words, as, with enlightened zeal and sanctified eloquence, he taught to Jew and Gentile the truth as it is in Jesus; proving to the Jews out of their own scriptures, even as Stephen had done, that the Mosaic Dispensation was the dispensation of preparation for the gospel of the Messiah, which he proclaimed.

On the return of Paul and Barnabas to Antioch, they found the peace of the church deeply disturbed by teachers who imperfectly comprehended the Gospel of Christ; and then, as later—for conceited ignorance is ever arrogant and dogmatic—narrow, precedent-following teachers withstood the breadth and simplicity of the gospel of Christ, as preached by Paul. The dissension was carried so far as to render it necessary to refer the matter to the apostles and elders at Jerusalem. A commission, consisting of Paul, Barnabas and certain others, was sent to Jerusalem to lay the matter before the mother church. When the commission reached Jerusalem, they were received of the church, the apostles, and the elders, to whom Paul and Barnabas declared all things which God had wrought by them; but those of the church still devoted to the ceremonial law, insisted that it was necessary to observe the law of Moses, in order to be saved. Bigotry is of one essence under all creeds and in all ages.

Subsequently the apostles and elders came together to consider the matter. After much disputing, St. Peter declared unto them how he had been taught of

God to put no difference between Jew and Gentile, deducing therefrom that it would be contrary to the will of God to put the yoke of the law on them, who had believed from among the Gentiles. Amidst the silence of the assembly, Paul and Barnabas arose and recounted the thrilling scenes of Paphos, Perga, Lystra, Derbe, and other points in the journey they had but lately made. Their recital hushed all opposition; they sat down, and in the hush of dispute, St. James arose and gave sentence. "We trouble not them, who, from among the Gentiles, are turned to God; we only require that they abstain from all pollution."

According to tradition, St. James, in outward aspect, was like unto an ancient prophet; his features were austere, he wore a white linen ephod, and walked with unshodden feet, and his hair and beard were unshorn; and he spoke with such earnest and commanding power that his sentence was the decree of the church.

The decision of the council having ended the controversy, Barnabas and Paul—and chosen men sent with them—returned to Antioch, taking with them the decree of the council of Jerusalem, which guaranteed to the churches a far-reaching Christian freedom. Based as the decree is on principles of universal application, it involved much more than relief from the pressure of any special rite or ceremony; it was indeed a charter of religious liberty to the young churches.

After remaining a while in Antioch, Barnabas and Paul projected a second missionary journey, but the contention as to the reliability of Mark as a fellow-missionary waxed so sharp, they parted asunder. Barnabas took Mark and sailed unto Cyprus. Paul chose Silas, one of the chosen men sent from Jerusalem, and they went through Syria, Cilicia, and other countries, confirming the churches and adding to their numbers.

At Lystra, the young Timothy, St. Paul's son in the gospel, joined him and Silas. After reaching Troas, it becomes evident from the narrative, that St. Luke joined the company, probably not only as fellow-missionary, but also as the beloved physician, to care for the infirm health of St. Paul.

Troas was classic-ground, but St. Paul was so possessed, and absorbed by his great mission, that its classic interest lay in the dark back-ground; his vision of the night reveals the deep workings of his soul. Straightway, St. Luke says, which must mean betimes in the morning,—Paul and his little company were seeking a vessel to convey them to the Macedonian shore.

After a voyage of two days they landed at Neapolis, the seaport of Philippi, the chief city of that part of Macedonia, and a Roman colony. On the morning of the first Sabbath after their arrival in Philippi, St. Luke writes, "we went forth without the gate, by a river side, where we supposed there was a place of prayer, and we sat down and spake unto the women which were come together." Only women were gathered at that chosen place of prayer. The fact that not a man of the house of Jacob was present on the Sabbath day, at the place chosen for the worship of the God of Israel, is sad to consider, and can only be accounted for as the result of an imperial edict issued shortly before, under which every man known to be a Jew was to be banished from Rome, and from her colonies.

But among the women, the seed sown on that Sabbath day fell on good ground, and brought forth abundant fruit. Lydia, the first Christian convert in Europe, besought her teachers to come and abide in her house; and from that household grew up the faithful church of Philippi, which once and again ministered to the wants of their father in Christ, when in a Roman dungeon he was awaiting sentence of death. Some of the incidents of St. Paul's stay in Philippi are full of interest; in that city lived the possessed maiden, who day after day followed the Christian teachers, declaring them to be servants of the Most High God, proclaiming the way of salvation; her continuous crying out touched the feeling heart of St. Paul, and in the name of Jesus he healed the pythonic madness of the maiden. To her masters, her frenzied soothsaying had brought much money, and the loss of their gain so angered them, that they dragged Paul and Silas into the market place, before the rulers of the city, on the utterly false charge of being disturbers of the peace; whereupon the rulers ordered that they should be beaten with rods and then cast into prison, and their feet made fast in the stocks.

Though bruised and sore from the cruel beating and in the most uncomfortable position, these brave, undaunted men of God prayed and sang praises to God through the slowly passing watches of the night. Such strange and soothing sounds hushed the prisoners into eager listening, but from this most unusual condition they were suddenly aroused by a dread convulsion of nature. Lo! the stillness of the midnight air is broken by the awful roar of a great earthquake, the foundations of the prison are shaken, the massive bolts fall out of place, the doors fly open, and every one's bands are loosed.

The jailer, aroused from sleep by the terrible alarm, is yet more terrified at finding the prison doors open; he draws his sword and is about to plunge it in his heart, supposing his prisoners had fled, when the loud voice of Paul assured him: "We are all here."

Revulsion of feeling as a flood must have swept over that jailer.

He called for lights, sprang in, and trembling from fear, fell before Paul and Silas.

He took them the same hour of the night and brought them to his house, and washed their stripes, asking, "What must I do to be saved?" And they spoke the word of the Lord unto him, and to all that were in his house; meat was set before the bruised and hungry apostles, and the Philippian jailer rejoiced greatly with all his house, believing in God.

When it was day the rulers sent, saying, "Let those men go." But St. Paul stands on his vantage ground of Roman citizenship. "Men who are Romans, uncondemned, have been publicly beaten; they shall not cast us out privily, let them come and bring us out." The sergeants repeated these words to the rulers, and the petty rulers were afraid when they heard the prisoners were Romans. In that case they had set at naught the majesty of Roman law, and to violate that law was not only to risk place, but life.

The rulers came and besought them, and when they brought them out they asked them to go away from the city.

Paul and Silas went to the house of Lydia, and when they had seen the brethren and comforted them, they took their departure, going through Amphipolis and Apollonia, to Thessalonica, where for three Sabbaths St. Paul went into the synagogue and reasoned with the Jews. But the riot of a brutal mob caused the city to loose the blessing of his continued labors; he left them by night, and journeyed to Berea.

The Jews of Berea, who came within the circle of St. Paul's acquaintance, were of a higher order of mind and manner than those of Thessalonica; the Berean Jews searched the scriptures to see if those things affirmed by Paul were so. And in Berea many Greeks believed, and of chief women, not a few. But the narrow and cruel bigotry of the Thessalonican Jews drove them to Berea, where they stirred up the multitude.

The church, fearing violence to their beloved apostle, immediately sent him forth with brethren who were to accompany him as far as the sea. But these brethren did not leave him to embark alone, they made the voyage with him, saw him safely in Athens, where he intended to await the coming of Silas and Timothy from Berea.

CHAPTER V.

Paul in Athens.

The scholarly Paul in Athens,—classic Athens, the most ancient and most renowned city of Greece, the mother of European Poetry, of Philosophy and of Art. Greek literature was not unknown to him, and the triumphs of Greek art were all about him; before him was the matchless Parthenon, and its magnificent statue of Athene, made of gold and ivory, and twenty-six cubits high. No doubt St. Paul had often to put up his hand to shield his weak eyes from the dazzling light flashing from the colossal and brilliant statue. But his whole being was so absorbed in his great mission that the most perfect specimen of highest art failed to impress him as did the simple altar, *To the Unknown God*.

Each day in the market place he taught and reasoned with the Athenians and strangers, who thronged the public places, eager to tell or to hear some new thing. From among the philosophers some of the Epicureans and of the Stoics encountered him; they desired to know of the doctrine more connectedly and intelligently than they could learn in the market place, in the midst of the babbling crowd, so they took hold of him and brought him to the Areopagus.

Though subject, Athens was shorn of her political greatness, yet the prestige of this famous Court was so great that the Areopagus continued to command the reverence of Athenians.

St. Paul is placed in the midst of the Areopagus. He stands before the august assembly with grave mien and dignified bearing; the assembly sits in respectful silence to hear the setting forth of his strange doctrine. As is his wont, he motions with his hand and in quiet, clear, incisive tones begins by saying, "Ye men of Athens, in all things I perceive that ye are too religious, for as I passed along observing the many objects of your worship, I found an altar with the inscription, 'To the Unknown God.' That unknown God whom ye worship in ignorance, Him declare I unto you. The God who dwelleth not in temples made with hands. The God who giveth to all men life, breath, and all things needful; the God who hath made of one blood every nation of men to dwell on all the face of the earth. The God who draweth all men that they may feel after Him, and find Him, though He is not far from each one of us." By the exquisite adaptation of his exordium he gently leads his hearers away from polytheism and follows it up by quoting from certain of their own poets to prove that we are the offspring of God; and he brings home the conclusion that beings conscious of feeling, of the power of thought, and of volition, should not esteem the Godhead from whom they have their being, to be like unto gold or silver, or sculptured stone; the times of such ignorance had passed. The apostle proceeds to speak of repentance, of righteousness, of judgment, and of the resurrection of the dead. When the skeptics heard of the resurrection of the dead they mocked, but the better part of the assembly said, "We will hear thee concerning this yet again." But there is no record of another audience of philosophers desiring to know of the doctrine he taught.

Simple and brief as was the great speech on Mars Hill, it was seed sown on good ground, we read that certain men clave unto him, among whom was Dionysius the Areopagite. St. Paul's stay in Athens does not seem to have brought forth the like immediate results as in many other cities, but that it produced enduring fruit we may learn from St. Origen, who speaks of a church in Athens as being greatly praised in the vineyard of the Lord. And with Pastor Bungener we may say that "the speech of St. Paul on Mars Hill, unfinished as it was, has nevertheless been a great page in the history of religion, of philosophy, and of humanity."

From Athens St. Paul went to Corinth, a city so beautiful for situation it has been called "The Star of Hellas," and so great was its commerce it was also called "The Bride of the Sea," and a distinguished modern writer speaks of Corinth as "The Vanity Fair of the Roman Empire." In Corinth Timothy joined his beloved father in the gospel, and brought him welcome tidings of the faith and love of the Thessalonian church, to which church he had from Athens sent Timothy to establish and comfort the brethren concerning their faith.

In Corinth St. Paul made his home with Aquila and Priscilla, Jews of Pontus, who under an edict of the Emperor Claudius had been banished from Rome. Whether they were already Christians or were converted through St. Paul's ministry is not known, but it is known that subsequently Aquila was a zealous preacher of the gospel. The apostle numbers them both among his helpers in Christ. Aquila may have been a manufacturer of tents, and on being compelled to leave Rome chose Corinth for his abode on account of its superior business advantages, and the apostle, being of the same craft, labored with him, that he might not be chargeable to any man.

Corinth was the centre of trade and commerce to both the eastern and western portions of the Roman Empire, and hence a church planted in Corinth would possess unusual facilities for extending its influence to various parts of the Empire.

St. Paul began laying the foundation of the Corinthian church by reasoning every Sabbath in the synagogue, until compelled to desist by the opposition and blasphemy of the Jews. From henceforth he declares, "I will go unto the Gentiles."

So exasperated were the Jews against him they seized him and brought him before the judgment seat of Gallio on the charge of persuading men to worship contrary to the law of Moses; on hearing the charge Gallio was indignant, and drove the accusers from the hall of judgment. He would have borne with them had they charged against St. Paul the most venial crime, or any infringement of civil law, but he was not minded to be a judge in a matter which he regarded as a foolish Jewish superstition. The Greeks vented their indignation by beating Sosthenes, the ruler of the synagogue; but Gallio, the Stoic, cared for none of these things.

After remaining in Corinth for a year and a half St. Paul sailed into Syria, stopping only a day in Ephesus, being desirous to reach Jerusalem in time for the approaching feast. His visit must have been very brief. The record states, "He went up and saluted the church and went down to Antioch." Antioch was the parent church of the Gentile world. How long he remained in that city is not stated; the record says, "He spent some time in Antioch, and departed, going through the region of Galatia and Phrygia in order, strengthening the brethren."

Passing through the upper coasts, he came to Ephesus, where he found twelve men who had received only the baptism of John. St. Paul explained to them St. John's central doctrine, of belief in Him who should come after him; the men believed, and were baptised in the name of the Lord Jesus. And for the space of three months the apostles reasoned and persuaded in the synagogue as to the things concerning the kingdom of God, but when the disobedient and hardened in heart spoke evil of the Way before the multitude, he withdrew, and the disciples with him. And for the space of two years he reasoned daily in the school of Tyrannus, so that all who dwelt in Asia, both Jews and Greeks, heard the word of the Lord; and miracles of healing were wrought by the hands of Paul, and his fame became known to all, both Jews and Greeks, that dwelt in Ephesus.

Ephesus, though a Greek city, was mostly Asiatic in character, devoted to the worship of Diana and to the practice of magic. The magnificent temple of Diana, with its graceful Ionic columns, was not only the pride of the city, but one of the seven wonders of the world. The image it enshrined, unlike the perfection of form and beauty in the idols of Athens, was small and rudely carved. It may have been a meteoric stone, and hence the ground of the popular belief that it fell down from Jupiter. On the rude head, feet, and girdle of the goddess mystic characters were engraved; on these characters the priests of Diana prepared many and costly books, which were regarded with superstitious reverence, and were eagerly purchased and studied by the devotees of Diana. Among those who were converted by the ministry of St. Paul were not a few who owned those books, and who practiced curious arts. The converts to Christianity brought their books together and burned them; those books had cost 50,000 pieces of silver. That must have been a heavy blow to the priests of Diana. But it remained for the shrine-makers to excite a tumult; one, Demetrius, fearing the loss of his gains, gathered his fellow-craftsmen together and harangued them, until their excitable natures were filled with a fury, which spread like wildfire. Soon the whole city was a scene of mad confusion, some crying one thing, and some another, for the most part knew not wherefore they were come together.

The frenzied mob seized Gaius and Aristarchus, men of Macedonia, Paul's companions in travel, and rushed with one accord to the theatre. St. Paul was minded to enter and speak to the people, but his friends withheld him. Alexander, another companion of St. Paul's, was brought out of the multitude; he motioned with his hand, and would have made a defence unto the people, but they perceived he was a Jew, and the mob for about two hours cried out, "Great is Diana of the Ephesians." We may suppose the mob screamed their throats dry, as the town clerk after that outburst, succeeded in quieting the multitude so that he might speak to them in terms of moderation and good sense.

CHAPER VI.

The Arrest and Trial at Cesarea.

Not only from without did St. Paul have to endure perils and persecutions; within the church envy and prejudice were at work. His motives were impugned, his authority disputed, and his conduct misrepresented. Poor human nature, what a sad spectacle! But the brave-hearted apostle, though deeply grieved at the wrong that was done him, faltered not in his work; he again went the round of the churches he had planted, exhorting and strengthening them. On his return from this journey he sailed past Ephesus, and came to Miletus, from whence he sent to Ephesus and called the elders of the church, to whom he briefly and feelingly recounted his manner of life, and his work among them; he gave them his charge, and commended them to God, and the word of His grace. It was a tender and sad parting, doubly sad, from the impression on the mind of the apostle that they should behold his face no more.

St. Paul was anxious to be in Jerusalem on the day of Pentecost, and he desired to set himself right with the mother church at Jerusalem. Though dissuaded by friends and warned by a prophet, he held on his way in what he felt was the path of duty. And when he would not be persuaded, his friends ceased, saying: "The will of the Lord be done."

On the day following their arrival at Jerusalem St. Paul and his company went in unto James, and all the elders were present. After salutations, St. Paul rehearsed, one by one, the things which God had wrought by his ministry. Having heard the account they glorified God, but warned him of the danger in which he stood from the many thousands of believers who were still zealous of the law, and had been informed that he taught all Jews who were among the Gentiles to forsake Moses. James and the elders advised St. Paul to join four of their men who had taken a vow, to purify himself with them, be at charges for them, that they might shave their heads, so that those many zealot brethren might see that he walked orderly, keeping the law.

St. Paul accepted the advice of the elders; he possessed that catholicity of spirit, which prevented a feeling of repugnance to ceremonial observances, on which he set no saving value; for the sake of weak brethren he was willing to consort with the Nazarites and take part in their ancient ceremonial. But it was of no avail; before the seven days were fulfilled Jews from Asia saw him in the temple, and stirring up the multitude with the cry, "This is the man that teacheth all men against the law and this place," they laid hold on him and dragged him out of the temple, and would have killed him but for the chief captain, who having learned that all Jerusalem was in an uproar, forthwith took soldiers and centurions and ran down upon them, and took St. Paul out of their hands, demanding who he was and what he had done. Some shouted one thing, and some another; not being able to obtain any certain information, he commanded that the prisoner be brought into the Castle. The multitude following after, crying out, "Away with him."

St. Paul was about to be brought into the Castle when he spoke to the chief captain in Greek, who asked in surprise, "Dost thou know Greek? Art thou not the Egyptian who stirred up sedition and led out four thousand men of the Assassins into the wilderness?" The apostle answered, "I am a Jew of Tarsus, a citizen of no mean city, and I beseech thee, grant me leave to speak unto the people." The chief captain granted his request, and standing on the stair he motioned with his hand; the multitude below gave heed and were silent. St. Paul courteously requested them as fathers and brethren to hearken to the defence he was about to make unto them. In the Hebrew tongue he succinctly told of his birth and bringing up, then of his opposition to and persecution of the Nazarenes, of his commission to Damascus, and with strong, graphic touches he portrays the scene on the Damascan plain, and details his interview with Ananias. Passing over the intervening years he speaks of his return to Jerusalem, and of his trance in the temple, and of the commission of Jesus given in the temple, "Depart, for I will send thee far hence unto the Gentiles." At this point a frantic outburst of mad fury from the multitude drowned the voice, not over strong, and the chief captain, not understanding the Hebrew tongue, and supposing the outburst occasioned by some confession of crime, ordered the prisoner to be examined by scourging. But with admirable presence of mind the apostle turns to the centurion claiming his right as a Roman citizen. The centurion speaks to the chief captain, "Take heed what thou doest, this man is a Roman." The chief captain going to the prisoner, demands "Tell me, art thou a Roman?" Being answered "Yea," the chief captain adds, "With a great sum I obtained Roman citizenship." St. Paul replies, "I am a Roman born." The scourgers straightway departed, and the chief captain was afraid, because uncondemned he had bound a Roman. But being desirous to ascertain wherefore the Jews were so infuriated against the prisoner he commanded the chief priests and all the council to come together on the next day, and he brought Paul before them. With steadfast look, addressing the council as brethren he was beginning a respectful apology, when Ananias, the high priest, commanded a bystander to smite him on the mouth; whereupon the apostle courageously arraigned him for acting without law when sitting to judge under law.

It was evident that a just decision need not be expected from that tribunal, therefore St. Paul struck at once to the heart of the matter, declaring that he was called in question, "touching the hope and resurrection of the dead," affirming that as a Pharisee and the son of a Pharisee, he believed in the resurrection of the dead. Upon which arose a great clamor; some of the Pharisee scribes strove against his accusers, declaring they found no evil in the man. The discussion waxed so violent that the chief captain fearing his prisoner would be torn in pieces, took him by force from among them, and placed him in safety in the castle.

But the suffering saint was cheered in the night season; the same Jesus who was with him in the temple was with him in the castle, bidding him be of good cheer.

The discovery of a conspiracy in Jerusalem against the life of St. Paul prevented further examination in that city, and he was sent under the protection of a military guard to Cesarea, to Felix, the governor.

False accusers, among them Ananias, the high priest, and the Jewish orator, Tertullus, followed him to Cesarea. When the case was called Tertullus stood up as accuser; after flattering Felix he began his accusation by denouncing St. Paul as a pestilent fellow, a mover of insurrections, a ringleader of the sect of the Nazarenes, and a profaner of the temple. After the accuser sat down the governor motioned the accused to rise, whereupon St. Paul arose. After a brief and courteous exordium he proceeded to show how false were the accusations brought against him, defying his acccusers to show any wrong doing they had found in him, or any other ground of accusation, save his belief in the resurrection of the dead, which he had avowed before the council.

He was dismissed for the time; but after some days the governor came with his Jewish wife, and St. Paul was again summoned before his judgment seat, and he reasoned with such clearness and power on righteousness, temperance and judgment to come that the bribe-loving Felix trembled before him.

When Porcius Festus succeeded the dastardly Felix, the Jews endeavored to make him a tool by which they could wreak their murderous vengeance on St. Paul, but their stratagem failed to entrap the respecter of Roman law. When his judgment seat was set in Cesarea, accused and accusers were summoned before him. Again the unprincipled accusers laid grievous charges against the apostle, and again St. Paul's defence disclosed the baseness of the charges. Possibly, to conciliate the factious people, over whom he had been made governor, or more probably because he considered the whole matter to be, as Gallio had thought, mere questions of superstition, therefore a case more appropriate to the Jewish capital than to the Roman city of Cesarea, Festus asked of St. Paul whether he would consent to have the trial transferred to Jerusalem.

However reasonable the governor's proposal may have seemed to himself, St. Paul knew that conspiracy and murder would lurk on the way. Standing as he was, before Cæsar's judgment seat, he appealed unto Cæsar. The appeal could not be refused, yet not a charge against the prisoner had been substantiated; the governor had no certain thing to write the Emperor. He was sorely perplexed. And when a short time after, he received a visit of congratulation from King Agrippa and Berenice, he

THE ARREST AND TRIAL AT CESAREA.

was eager to consult with the king on his perplexing situation. King Agrippa desired to hear the man, whereupon Festus called together the chief captains and principal men of the city, and with much pomp they entered the hall of audience, whither St. Paul had been summoned. The whole company being duly seated, the governor turning to King Agrippa and his other guests, stated his wish that from the examination some certain accusation might be elicited worthy of being transmitted to the Emperor, it being a most unreasonable thing to send a prisoner to Rome not having any charge to prefer against him.

The apostle having received permission to speak, arose, and stretching forth his hand, began his defence. With appropriate courtesy addressing himself to Agrippa, who had given the permission to speak, he then proceeded to set forth the manner of his life from his youth up, which having been lived in Jerusalem, the Jews knew that he had been a Pharisee after the straightest sect. And, he continued, their persecutions are on account of my declaring, through a risen Jesus, the great Pharisee doctrine of the resurrection of the dead. He then went on to recapitulate in clear and incisive terms the persecutions, which in all good conscience he had perpetrated against the Way he now preached, and briefly related the remarkable events preceding and completing his conversion to Christ. And of his commission from the risen Jesus, as witness and minister to the Gentiles, that they might turn from darkness to light, from the power of Satan unto God. And for that cause, he emphatically declared, "the Jews assayed to kill me, though I testified only what the prophets and Moses did say should come, that Christ must suffer, should arise from the dead and proclaim light, both to the people and to the Gentiles."

At this point in his defence the governor interrupted, exclaiming in a loud voice, "Paul, thy much learning doth turn thee to madness!" "Most noble Festus," replies St. Paul, "I am not mad, I speak only the words of truth and soberness; the king knoweth of these matters, they were not done in a corner." Turning to Agrippa St. Paul makes a direct appeal, "King Agrippa, believest thou the prophets?" The eagle eye of Paul had been reading Agrippa's soul through the varying expressions of his countenance, for he immediately adds, "I know that thou believest." The answer of Agrippa affords proof that St. Paul was not mistaken. To that answer St. Paul replies, "Except these bonds I would to God that thou and all that hear me this day were not only almost but altogether such as I am."

What a sublime and measureless extent of wish, reaching up to the highest beatitude of Heaven, and limitless as eternity, and in this mortal life conferring the happiness of an unswerving faith under persecution, and which, in presence of death, can shout victory over death and the grave.

The governor and those who sat with him withdrew, and after consultation agreed that nothing deserving death or bonds was found against the prisoner. Agrippa declared that but for the prisoner's appeal to Cæsar he might be set at liberty. But from that appeal there was no retreat. St. Paul was delivered along with other prisoners to the custody of a centurion of the Augustan band.

CHAPTER VII.
St. Paul in Rome—Characteristics.

The voyage to Rome was long and fraught with many dangers; they were shipwrecked off the coast of Melita, but that appalling shipwreck, so graphically sketched by St. Luke, was a mercy to the people of the island.

In Rome the lenient treatment of St. Paul was in accordance with what might be expected from Roman justice toward a prisoner against whom had been preferred no charge of crime or violated law.

St. Paul remained in Rome two years, living in his own hired house, "receiving all who came unto him, preaching the kingdom of God and teaching the things concerning the Lord Jesus Christ, none forbidding him." At this point in the life of St. Paul the valuable record of St. Luke closes.

That he was acquitted may be learned from other sources and from his own writings. Five years or thereabouts are estimated to have elapsed between his acquittal and his final arrest; during those five years he made a journey into Spain, and was absent some two years, and from what some of the fathers say, he probably went as far as the isles of Britain.

On his return he resumed his apostolic round of work among the churches, reproving, exhorting and comforting them; and adding to their numbers.

His last letter, while yet a freeman of Rome, was written from Corinth shortly before leaving for Nicopolis, where he intended to winter. But alas! before the winter was over he was arrested and sent a prisoner to Rome. No lenient treatment now, no dwelling in his own hired house; the terrible charge of complicity with the incendiaries at Rome is brought against him, and also the charge of continuously violating the law, which prohibited the propagation of a new religion among Romans.

His trial on the first charge resulted in acquittal, no particle of proof could be found against him, but he was remanded back to prison to await his trial on the second charge.

Incarceration in a Roman prison was a hard fate, but the heart of the apostle exulted in the strength of triumphant faith; from that Roman prison he wrote his last letter, full of instruction, to his son in the gospel, closing with a burst of triumphant and unselfish faith, looking far as the race of man shall reach—"to all them that love the appearing of the Lord, the righteous judge." Then follow brief mention of men and matters, and that sad statement, "At my first trial no man stood with me, all men forsook me." With him as it had been with his Master.

From St. Paul's statement it is but fair to conclude that the faithful Luke had not then reached Rome; the beloved physician who ministered unto him and comforted him in prison would have stood with him at his trial. Later, in this last letter, he writes, "Only Luke is with me." Touching words, and they give to St. Luke, the able writer, the beloved physician, an added claim on Christian gratitude and love.

The traditional accounts of St. Paul's personal appearance are meagre, disparaging, and unreliable; possible a truer picture may be obtained by gathering materials from his writings, from those of St. Luke, and from his tireless activity, and remarkable power of endurance; and from these materials to let imagination outline a portrait. When entering upon his apostolic work she paints a young man of medium height, lithe of limb and supple in movement, readily springing through a window into a basket to be let down by the wall. That agile well-knit young man has a finely formed head admirably set on his shoulders, and the expression of his fine Jewish face bespeaks a man of action, a man of earnest convictions, of high moral purpose, unflagging energy, and superior intellectual power; deep set, dark and penetrating eyes complete the picture of the young man Barnabas presented to the church at Jerusalem.

But as the great apostle those graces attendant upon health and strength have disappeared; the years freighted with incessant labors, perils and persecutions have changed his outward aspect. He still stands erect, but the rounded limb, the agile movement are not there; the luminous eyes are weak and heavy, but their light is not quenched. When his spirit burns with holy zeal in disputation or in preaching, those weak, dim eyes brighten and glow with moral passion and the poetry of feeling, yea, with the fervor of inspired genius, and the feeble voice grows strong again as he reasons of the mystery of the will of God and the riches of His grace freely bestowed through the Beloved.

During those years of infirm health, struggling against sickness, perils and persecutions, he continues to declare unto Jew and Gentile the unsearchable riches of the gospel of Christ. Behold him as he rises to speak of "the depth of the knowledge and wisdom of God, of His judgments and ways past finding out." He stands weak, pale, emaciated, but his great soul gives him dignity of bearing, as with his peculiar and impressive motion of the hand he bespeaks the attention of his hearers. Those who love the glad tidings are attent to catch every precious word; but among those hearers are mockers, curious to see and hear the man whose letters they have found to be weighty and powerful, but they are blind to soul-greatness, and seeing the physical man almost a wreck they say, "His bodily presence is weak and his speech contemptible."

St. Paul's health must have considerably improved and his voice again become sonorous before his capture in Jerusalem, or from the top of the castle stair the power of his speech could not have hushed and held spell-bound the surging multitude below until the doctrine of the resurrection roused their senseless fury. Such power of voice could not at once have been called forth by stress of feeling, nor by the immediate action of his wonderful nerve-force which during the whole course of his apostleship enabled him to bear up under stripes and imprisonments; under perils by land and perils by sea, through his confidence of faith in Christ Jesus our Lord.

And this view of a physically improved condition preceding his arrest in Jerusalem is supported by a medallion likeness said to have been found in the ruins of Herculaneum, and thought to have been taken in the early part of his first Roman imprisonment. If the medallion is a genuine find it is a precious recovery and a valuable corrective of current notions in regard to the personal appearance of St. Paul. The picture shows a noble conformation of head and face of the handsomer Jewish type; the beard is full and flowing; the whole represents a care-worn, thoughtful man of mature years, and it pretty fairly satisfies the student of his life and writings. On the obverse side of the medallion the inscription is *Paulus vas electionis*. On the reverse side, in Latin, are the twenty-sixth and twenty-seventh verses of the sixty-eighth psalm, from the Septuagint. Verse twenty-sixth, "Praise ye God in your assemblies (or in the highest), even the Lord, from the fountains of Israel," verse twenty-seventh, "Here is Benjamine the youngest, their leader." The latter verse was evidently added in special compliment to the great Benjamite of the picture, whose face is that of a leader, thoughtful, determined and energetic.

But it is not necessary to seek the aid of medallion likenesses, nor the plastic fashioning of imagination to portray the spiritual man, whose unmistakable greatness is seen in the graphic touches of St. Luke, and in his own writings, which are the great store house of Christian doctrine. They give the mental measure of the man who could touch the profoundest chords of human feeling, and who could enter into the subtlest workings of the human intellect, and again, teach with a simplicity that all men may comprehend.

Both the writings and the conduct of St. Paul witness to an intense nature, in which cohere the opposite elements of gentleness and sternness, together with great strength of will and an unswerving loyalty to truth.

And he also possessed in a high degree a subtle power of abstraction; it is indeed the master-key to some of his grandest arguments. His long training in the school of Hillel may have developed the natural bent of his mind into a leading mental characteristic, to which may be attributed those things hard to be understood, which have baffled so many learned workers at exegetical crucibles, but which, under the warm light of intelligent Christian apprehension, cast off the hard crust of subtle abstraction and disclose the wholesome, spiritual fruit within.

The gentleness of St. Paul's nature is exquisitely shown in his letter to Philemon as he pleads in behalf of the erring but repentant and converted Onesimus; and his sternness is seen in his sharp and fearless rebuke of a brother apostle for a course of conduct which to him seemed a time-serving policy. And being himself so strong of purpose he was lacking in kindly sympathy to a weaker brother; he was hard on John Mark, and thus brought about a separation from his faithful and long time co-worker, Barnabas. But whether gentle or stern he was ever loyal to his conception of right.

CHAPTER VIII.

THE EPISTLES OF ST. PAUL.

In his epistles St. Paul bequeathed to the church an invaluable treasure; they are a very temple of Christian doctrine on whose corner-stone he inscribed the immortal words, "As many as are led by the spirit of God, these are the sons of God." "The spirit bearing witness with our spirit, that we are the children of God, and if children, then heirs, heirs of God and joint heirs with Christ." These precious words declare to all men of every race and nation that the church of our God and His Christ is the church universal, whose portals are open to all men who seek after righteousness and holiness after

"a larger life in service
To man, for love of God."

Under the ordering of the providence of God the ages, as they move on from renaissance to renaissance, will bring an ever enlarging sphere of thought and of knowledge, and men will attain a clearer apprehension of the sublime simplicity of the gospel of Christ as preached by St. Paul, they will find that the writings of St. Paul will not support the subtilely wrought, yet cumbrous superstructure of Christian philosophy which has been reared upon them. Men will learn to distinguish between his setting forth of the truth as it is in Jesus, and his illustrative and abstract arguments, arguments often based on his intense Hebraism, and on those beliefs and traditions of his times, concerning which he charges the church of Thessalonica, "Hold fast the traditions which ye were taught, whether by word or letter of ours."

Of the letters of St. Paul thirteen have come down

to us. These thirteen precious documents are the earliest writings of the New Testament. Nine of them were written to the churches; they all touch the same key-note, and in some of them it reaches full rounded chords; that key-note is the liberty wherewith Christ has made us free, free from the Levitical or ceremonial law.

St. Paul's epistles invariably open with words of loving greeting, and generally there follows a thanksgiving to God on behalf of those to whom he is writing and to whom he is about to declare some great Christian truths, and the application of these truths to daily life.

The epistles of St. Paul comprise about one fourth of the New Testament; the oldest, the first written, are those to the church in Thessalonica; these letters were written about A. D. 53, while on his second missionary journey. Some five years or more elapsed before he wrote again to the churches. His next letters were written to the Corinthian church, and during his third missionary journey he wrote the epistle to the Galatians, and the epistle to the Romans.

The hypothesis that St. Paul's thorn in the flesh was a sore disease of the eyes finds some support in his words to the Galatians. Probably his eyes were never strong after that severe stroke of blindness without the gate of Damascus. He writes to the Galatians, "That which was a temptation to you in my flesh ye despised not nor rejected, but received me as an angel of God, even as Christ Jesus. For I bear you witness that if possible ye would have plucked out your own eyes and given them to me." Sore eyes, inflamed and festering, are to many people a temptation to turn away from, if not to despise and reject the sufferer.

The epistle to the Galatians, with its clarion cry of liberty, through knowledge of the truth, the truth as it is in Christ, was a special favorite with Luther; he called it "My epistle, my constant friend and companion."

The epistle to the Romans deals with some of the most profound problems that have ever been presented to the human mind. It has been called "The Kernel of the New Testament," and it has given rise to more disputation than any other portion of the sacred writings. St. Paul has been made responsible for much that he evidently never meant.

His great doctrine of salvation by faith has from the early ages of the church, even to these latter days, been declared to be in direct opposition to the doctrine of St. James; but to the student of the two epistles the opposition or difference is found to be only an apparent difference growing out of the different standpoints of the two apostles, and the consequent difference of their method of presenting the same great truth, for the faith which St. Paul preaches is not a passive faith, but an active life-principle, bringing forth the fruits of love to God and man, as may be seen in his life, which was literally crammed full of good works, through which his faith shines clear and bright as the morning star. His life witnesses that the two apostles are essentially at one.

During St. Paul's first imprisonment at Rome he wrote the letters to the Philippians, to Philemon, to the Colossians, and the letter to the Ephesians. This letter is the last utterance of St. Paul to the Gentile church, and is the crowning glory of his writings. "A divine letter, glowing with the flame of Christian love, and the splendor of holy light, and flowing with fountains of living water."

In the earlier ages of the church, and in the later times the epistle to the Ephesians has been thought to be the letter written to the Laodiceans, to which the apostle refers in his letter to the Colossians.

The letter contains strong internal evidence that it was not written exclusively to the church in Ephesus, a church with which St. Paul has been long and intimately associated. Most probably this letter was, as suggested by Canon Farrar, a "circular letter to the churches of Asia." "And this," he says, "accounts for the exclusion of all private salutations, and for the absence of affectionate intimacy and personal appeal by which it is marked." Tertullian and other church fathers to the time of Jerome, state that the old copies of this epistle had no address; the superscription, "To the Ephesians," was added on the margin of the later manuscripts.

Of the three pastoral epistles, the first letter to Timothy, and the letter to Titus, are believed to have been written after St. Paul's liberation from his first imprisonment in Rome, and during his last missionary journey. In his former missionary journeys Timothy had generally been with him, but now he must be at his post as overseer or bishop of the church in Ephesus, and St. Paul writes to instruct, to strengthen, and to encourage him, that he may be the more fully fitted for the rightful discharge of his important duties as a minister of Christ.

As St. Paul's last visit to Ephesus was drawing to a close, in the autumn preceding his final arrest, he wrote his masterly letter to Titus, whom he urges to join him at Nicopolis, where he had proposed to winter.

The last letter of St. Paul which has come down to us, is the second letter to Timothy. This letter was written during his final imprisonment at Rome, while he was awaiting his last trial with no expectation of acquittal. With death staring him in the face he still felt an earnest heart-hunger to see and to embrace again his beloved son in the gospel. In this touching letter he urges Timothy to come to him with all possible speed, assigning as the reason that the time of his departure was at hand.

This last letter of the great apostle, The Chosen Vessel of Christ, glows with the light of triumphant faith, and to this day it touches in the hearts of his spiritual children the same thankful yet sorrowing chord which it struck in the bosom of Timothy.

The trial of St. Paul came sooner than he had expected; for the cloke, for the books, for the special parchments he had left at Troas he had no further need. But the speedier trial and sentence of death did not find him unprepared; he was ready to be offered up. His strong faith was exultant in its firm grasp of the promise of life which is in Christ Jesus, whose apostle he was by the will of God; and that faith enabled him to realize that his death day in time would be his coronation day in eternity.

Sentence of condemnation was pronounced against him, but as a Roman citizen he was spared the lingering torture of death by crucifixion; under Roman law a Roman might not be nailed to a tree.

The place of execution lay outside the gate of the imperial city. To the death place, surrounded by a cohort of Roman soldiers, the dauntless apostle is led. They lay bare the neck, he kneels, his head is placed on the fatal block, the headsman raises his sword, it falls, a blinding flash of light from the polished steel, and all is over. In the practiced hand of the Roman executioner one terrible stroke of the sharp sword, and that noble head is severed from the emaciated body. A sharp, swift passage from the church militant to the church triumphant. A blessed exchange from the company of Roman jailers and Roman soldiers to "the glorious company of the apostles, to the noble army of martyrs, to the presence of Him who didst open the kingdom of heaven to all believers."

PART II.

CHAPTER IX.

THE PRIMITIVE CHURCH.

No marble column nor massive arch nor tower of stone was erected to commemorate the invaluable labors of St. Paul. But the church in Europe, founded and builded up in the Christian faith by him and his little company of co-laborers, is his enduring, his living monument. The influence of the church he planted shaped the destiny of Europe. The church brought western Europe to the forefront of the nations of the world.

After the death of St. Paul the church in Europe, for many years, continued to be an indefatigable body of Christian workers. And indeed during the age of the apostolic fathers the church in general was one great household in the faith. All Christians, without regard to racial or social distinctions, were bound by the bonds of Christian faith and love into one great brotherhood. But succeeding ages brought into the church controversies, contentions, and bitter strifes; and later, when the shield of temporal power protected the church against persecution, she was yet more deeply wounded in her spiritual life by worldly vanity and pride, by lust of power and greed of wealth and rank. And, moreover, Christianity was sorely wounded in the house of her friends by narrow and cruel misconceptions of duty, and by the arrogance of ignorance.

The amount of error, of crime, which in the course of ages crept stealthily into the church, was sufficient to have utterly destroyed her, but for her divine vitality, which was ever, in her most degenerate days, attested through faithful witnesses who stood up for the truth as it is in Christ Jesus. But for those loyal and devoted men, women and children the church must have perished, even as dynasties and empires have perished through their degeneracy.

In the days of her primitive purity, when the whole church was one great commune, that branch of the church in Rome was specially zealous of good works. In Rome the gospel of Christ won its way into all classes of society. The captives and hostages held in the imperial city were not overlooked, and many of them gladly accepted the gospel of consolation from the lips of the loving-hearted messengers of Christ. And when those Christian hostages were redeemed and the Christian captives exchanged or set free, they became to their people preachers and teachers of that gospel which in the days of their distress had brought to them comfort and consolation.

The Roman church, so zealous in good works, grew and multiplied, and became the leading one of the households of the faith in Europe. Her converts were drawn from all ranks of society, from among the nobles, the philosophers, the army, the merchants, and the slaves. All of these were influenced more or less largely by the exemplary lives of the Christians as seen in their daily conduct; under all circumstances, in peace and under persecution, those striking traits which never fail to touch appreciative hearts were found among Christians. They abounded in brotherly love and in kindness to everyone, even to enemies, and in temperance, patience, and every good work.

The converts, both of the clergy and laity, labored with fervent zeal for the extension of the good cause. And such great success crowned their labors that in the second century Irenæus writes, "The gospel was carried into Lybia and Egypt, to the Celts, Iberians and Germans." He further states "That the gospel was carried to the ends of the earth, and that the people were glad to accept it, for it met and satisfied all the religious cravings of the human soul."

Such marvelous success was not owing to outward advantages, for Christianity as a *religio-nova*,--a new religion,—was under the proscription of the Roman law. The death penalty was paid by St. Paul as propagator of a new religion among Romans.

During his life there were many Christians in Cæsar's household, and from that time on, Christians continued to hold important positions at the imperial court and in the army, although hostile laws were enacted against them, and at times they fell victims to these laws, they were cast out of their positions and suffered cruel persecutions.

The persecutions of Christians under Nero were long and cruel, and only partially ceased with his death. In those early ages of our era, Christians could have no feeling of safety, tumults and persecutions were so frequently aroused against them. But when they were favored with seasons of respite they labored earnestly in season and out of season to make known the way of life, and their labors, as at first, were crowned with success. After the accession of Domitian to the imperial throne a fierce persecution broke out against them, though it was not of long continuance. The Emperors of the second century were less cruel, and the Christian church through thousands of channels spread over many countries, and Christianity began to permeate the whole fabric of social and political life.

The church had, as one great brotherhood, ignored all political, social and ethnic barriers. The only distinctions recognized were those of *Christian* and *non-Christian*. And each local church or congregation was independent of every other, governed only by its bishop or elder, and possessing its own common treasury. But during the second century a more complex organization began to develop; churches in the same province met in deliberative assemblies. These assemblies led to an increase of the power of the bishops, and finally to the elevation of the bishop of the chief city of a province to the rank of superior or presiding bishop. This was the first step toward the overthrow of primitive congregational church government. By Greek writers these deliberative assemblies are called Synods, by Latin writers Councils.

In the third century the bishops of Antioch and of Alexandria claimed precedence over all other eastern bishops, and the bishop of Rome claimed supremacy over all western bishops.

The provincial assemblies or councils soon developed into general councils; eventually the whole form of church government was changed, and the simplicity of Christian fellowship was destroyed. But notwithstanding the evil of her secularized government the church continued to grow; she extended her boundaries both in the east and in the west. In her communion she had hosts of spiritually minded men and women, whose earnest zeal and holy lives were a force not to be withstood, and on the other hand the awe of the invisible world, and of its rewards and punishments, as taught by Christians, drew multitudes into the Christian fold. But a fearful trial of their faith was in store for them. The terrible persecution under Diocletian, early in the fourth century, reduced the church almost to dire extremity. Their scriptures were burned, and their church edifices were demolished.

This direful persecution was declared by some of the church fathers to be a judgment sent from God upon the church as a chastisement on account of their angry contentions concerning doctrines, and their worldly wranglings about precedence and rank. Such contentions had torn the church into bitter factions; it stands recorded that "the abusive epithets were as darts and spears which Christians hurled against Christians." But these bitter revilings were silenced for a time by the Diocletian persecution. It was a time that tried men's souls. Under cruel torture some of the Christians abjured their faith and saved their lives, but a far larger number were brave and true of heart; holding fast to their faith they passed through the gate of martyrdom to the life everlasting.

The church came out of that persecution weak and crippled, but Christians were drawn closer together; they strengthened and comforted each other in that dark hour of need when the catacombs and other secret places had to be sought for worship. But this darkest hour, when it meant death to be known as a Christian, was followed by the break of the day of deliverance.

The young Emperor of the West, Constantine, son of parents friendly to Christianity, was marching against Maxentius, who had entrenched himself in Rome.

As the army of Constantine neared the city he commanded a halt, that his men might have a brief rest. During that hour of rest Constantine beheld in the heavens a wonderful sign, the sign of the cross, and above it he saw the appearance of certain characters, in which he read, "In this shalt thou conquer." To him it was a token sent from God, and as such he pointed it out to his army. The men beheld the sign, and were filled with faith in the promised victory. Constantine and his army resumed their march, full of wondering faith in the sign they had seen, and went into action in the full flush of belief that victory would perch on their banners.

THE PRIMITIVE CHURCH. 63

The battle was fought and the expected victory was gained; a victory which made Constantine supreme sovereign of the western empire. As an expression of his gratitude to God he issued an edict proclaiming unrestrained liberty of worship to all Christians. He rebuilt the churches which had been razed to their foundations, and at his own expense he had many new and elegant churches erected. And without delay he enacted a law that all Christians held in slavery should forthwith be released.

And throughout his empire the infliction of death by crucifixion was peremptorily forbidden. The cross was never again to be used as an instrument of death; it was henceforth to be borne before his legions as a symbol of triumph.

His victory over Licinius, Emperor of the Roman empire in the East, A. D. 324, made him sole Emperor over all the great Roman empire, and thereafter he is known to history as Constantine the Great. And Christianity under the shadow of the imperial ægis could both work and rest in peace; no more dread forebodings, no more enduring of destroying persecutions. And the no longer despised Christians grew rapidly into a numerous and important body in the political world.

But alas! the spiritual condition of the church is sad to behold; she was torn by the bitterness of controversies and denunciations, which again as darts and spears sorely wounded the peace of the church. Constantine was deeply grieved at such a condition of the church, and he thought it to be his duty as temporal head of the church to take measures which he deemed sufficient to cast out of the church the apples of discord. Acting upon this conception of his duty he sent letters of invitation to the bishops of every province of the Roman empire, to meet in council in the city of Nicæ, in Asia Minor.

Nicæ was an important and accessible city, alike

convenient to the bishops of the east and of the west. In May, A. D. 325, three hundred and eighteen bishops assembled in Nicæ, and priests, deacons and laymen increased the numbers of the council to two thousand. After the bishops, the two most prominent persons connected with the council were Athanasius, a young deacon of Alexandria, and the presbyter Arius the Libyan. Foremost among the vexed questions which the council was to consider and decide were the doctrines set forth by Arius, and known as Arianism. The matter was discussed to some extent before the formal opening of the Council by the Emperor, who did not arrive until the 14th of June.

When it was announced to the Council that the Emperor had arrived, all business was laid over, the bishops took their seats and in silence awaited his appearance in the Council. This was announced by Christian heralds, whereupon all present arose to receive his Imperial Majesty.

The great church historian, Eusebius, bishop of Cesarea, who was an eye witness, says: "The Emperor appeared as a messenger from God. He is a tall man of magnificent figure, but full of grace and humility; he walked up to the golden seat which had been prepared for him with eyes reverently downcast. Having seated himself, the bishop on his right—most probably the historian himself—addressed him in a brief oration." In which oration the bishop thanked God for having given to the church and to the world such an Emperor. And again there was silence,—the Emperor then arose and formally opened the Council with an appropriate speech. In closing he said, "When I learned of the divisions and contentions which tore the church I felt convinced that I ought not to delay in giving attention to a matter of so great importance, and it is from the desire of being useful to the church that I have convened this great Council. But I shall not believe that my end is attained until I see that peace and that union reign among you, which you are commissioned as the appointed of the Lord to preach to others. Do not hesitate, my friends, ye servants of God, to banish from among you all causes of dissension, by solving controversial difficulties, according to the law of peace, and so accomplish a work well pleasing to God; a work that will be a great joy to me, your fellow servant in the Lord." The Emperor then gave place to the presidents of the Council.

From the time of the imperial opening to the formulating of the Nicene creed we have but few sources of information as to the manner of deliberation, but from what we have it is clearly evident that the spirit of peace did not rest upon the Council. Eusebius says, "Grievances were numerous on both sides, orthodox and Arian. There were from the beginning many controversies, accusations and replies." From other sources we learn that for several days memorials were sent to the Emperor, bishops accusing brother bishops, and laymen criminating bishops. A day was set apart in order to decide these grievances. When the Emperor entered the Council on that day he held in his hand a package sealed with his signet. "These," said he, "are the complaints of brethren which have been sent to me. I have not read one of them." And thereupon he threw the package in the fire.

The Council continued in session until the latter part of August. It condemned Arianism, anathematized Arius and his friends, and passed sentence of banishment against them. It settled the time of keeping Easter, though the disagreement as to the period of Easter did not at once disappear after the decision of the Nicene Council. Other doctrinal questions and church schisms were deliberated and decided upon, and twenty canons were drawn up and approved.

But the great work of the Council was the formulating of the Nicene creed as the general expression of the faith of the church. The Emperor gave his full approval to the creed. It was signed by all the bishops, except five, and in order to compel unity of action in the Council the Emperor threatened to banish any bishop who did not sign the creed. Three of the bishops who had refused reconsidered the matter and signed; the remaining two bishops, Secundus and Theonas, pleaded conscientious scruples and refused to sign, even in the face of banishment. The Emperor forthwith executed his threat, and passed sentence of banishment against them, and against all priests who sided with them.

But none of these measures brought peace to the church. Her divisions could not be healed by creeds nor canons; neither by decrees nor sentences of banishment. The true peace of the church can only be attained through Faith, Hope and Love, through the Christ likeness.

CHAPTER X.

The Bishop of Rome.

From the famous Council of Nicæ may be dated the desire in the western or European church for a definite constitution to be held and obeyed as a binding and sacred obligation, and for a sole head of the church as an external representative of the unity resulting from that sacred obligation. From this desire on the religious or churchly side originated the papacy or universal fatherhood of the bishop of Rome. On the temporal side papal pre-eminence grew out of the unsound condition of the times.

After Constantine removed the seat of government from Rome to Byzantium, which he renamed Constantinople, the bishop of Rome was the most important person remaining in the ancient city, and to him the people looked as chief ruler. The position was a responsible and difficult one, for the people of Rome had through long-continued luxury and sensuality become enervated and debauched.

There was no longer a sturdy middle class, the sure reliance of the state, as there had been under the Republic and under the early empire. The military, the nobles, and the servile plebeians made up the population, which was turbulent and lawless, incapable of defending themselves against the barbarians who over-ran the country and threatened even "the ancient citadel."

The sack of Rome, under Alaric the Goth, A. D. 415, struck terror into the people, who had been supinely relying on their ancient prestige.

At Hippo, St. Augustine bewailed the sack of Rome by barbarians as the end of all human power and glory. He thought the fall of Rome presaged the end of the world. But so far from the fears of St. Augustine being realized, the sack of the city did not put an end to even the nominal empire. That shade of an empire continued to abide at Rome, though Attila and his Huns devastated Italy almost to the gates of the imperial city, and continued to live, though Genseric the Vandal took the city, and for fourteen days continued the horrors of the sack; but that shade of empire vanished at the coming of Theodoric the Goth. Theodoric, son of a Gothic king, was, while a youth, held as a hostage at Constantinople and won such favor with the Emperor that he caused him to be trained as his son at arms, but royal favor could not bribe Theodoric's stout Gothic heart. The military training of the Greeks was drilled into him, but the intellectual training was either withheld or Theodoric despised it and would not learn.

On the return of Theodoric to his people he took command of the Gothic army and trained his men according to the discipline he had learned at Constantinople; at the same time he strove to hold them to a higher sense of justice and of uprightness than he had found in the imperial army. Rome, all Italy fell before the stout arms of the brave Goths, and Theodoric became king of Italy.

In his history of Florence, speaking of that period, Machiavelli says, "Theodoric possessed great talents, both for war and peace; in war he was always conqueror, and in peace he conferred great benefits upon the people under him. He enlarged Ravenna and restored Rome, and wholly by the force of his character he kept within their proper bounds all the barbarian kings who occupied the empire." By force of character, wisdom and virtue Theodoric held not only Rome and Italy, but every part of the western empire in lawful obedience, and the country, freed from the continual invasions of the barbarians, acquired new vigor and began to live in an orderly and civilized manner; and from the mixed population arose new languages, as may be seen in the similar yet differing languages of Italy, of France, and of Spain; "these dialects or languages partaking of the native idioms of the new people and of the old Roman formed a new manner of discourse."

As the first to put a stop to many evils Theodoric deserves the highest praise, as during the thirty-eight years he reigned in Italy "he brought," says Machiavelli, "the country to such a state of greatness that her previous sufferings were no longer recognizable."

Theodoric established the seat of his empire at Ravenna, but he allowed the church of Rome to take precedence of the church of Ravenna, and hence the popes acquired greater importance in the affairs of Italy, "but not until the coming of the Lombards did the popes have any other authority than what grew out of reverence for their habits and doctrine." Machiavelli further states that "under the pontificate of Pascal I., the priests of the church of Rome from being near the pope and attending the elections of the pontiffs began to dignify their power with a title by calling themselves Cardinals, and arrogating to themselves great authority."

After the death of Theodoric the Great, the east Gothic war nearly destroyed the prosperity of Theodoric's long reign of thirty-eight years. Rome was again reduced to such a degenerate state that it bordered on anarchy; all authority except the papal authority was entirely disregarded.

The pope and the clergy were the only organic remnants of the Roman empire, and in addition to this prestige was the popular belief that the pope possessed a reserve of spiritual power. The awe of the supernatural was a potent influence among all classes of society from princes to peasants.

On the death of Pope Pelagius II., A. D. 590, the better class of people saw clearly the necessity of having a brave, firm man as their chief ruler, and on several occasions the archdeacon of Rome had shown himself to be just such a brave, firm man as was needed in the unsettled state of affairs both in church and state.

Without any effort on his part the archdeacon was elected to the papacy, and was consecrated as Gregory the First, and is known to history as Gregory the Great. His government fulfilled the expectations of the people and of the church. He restored order in the city, and through wise and conciliatory measures averted the dreaded scourge of invasions.

He would not sanction the attempt to spread Christianity through force of arms; he taught that the gospel of peace must be enforced through peaceful measures; and he labored to banish the abuses which were constantly creeping into the church.

That he did not claim to be the supreme head of the church militant is evident from his rebuke to the bishop of Constantinople for arrogating to himself such a claim. Pope Gregory First is reported to have declared that a bishop made himself anti-Christ by claiming to be universal Bishop. But the successors of Gregory the Great were not like minded. They departed further and further from the course he pursued. They strove for princely power and splendor; they multiplied rights and ceremonies until the simplicity of worship was well-nigh lost.

Externally the church was great and powerful, but because of spiritual barrenness she was powerless to turn her people from sensuous pleasures. The literature of the age was as degenerate as the church and the community, and for this the church was chiefly culpable, not only on account of her degenerate condition but also through her unwise prohibition of liberal learning. Even Gregory the Great contemned all secular learning, and all music save church music. For a priest to sing, except in church service, he regarded as levity and sin. It would have been his good pleasure to see all books of Greek and Latin learning committed to the flames.

CHAPTER XI.

THE EARLY MONKS.

FORTUNATELY, even in the age of the good pope, and all through the succeeding ages, there were some broader minded men, especially among the monks, who had a deeper insight into the needs of human nature, and a truer conception of Christianity.

To the indefatigable labors of the early monks Europe is largely indebted for her salvation from barbarism. Monks, through their self-sacrificing missionary enterprises, opened the way for the subsequent civilization of western Europe. They cleared the wild lands which had been given to them, they cultivated them and made them fruitful. They built monasteries, and by frugality and prudent management they acquired sufficient wealth to build hospitals in which the sick and indigent were cared for, and they founded schools. Among the people schools had mostly been allowed to die out, and the books of ancient learning would have been lost but for their preservation in the monasteries.

Learning was kept alive in Italy only in the monastic and cathedral schools. The attendance at the schools in those early ages was generally small; there were but few other students than those intended for the church as the whole course of instruction was in Latin, and Latin was no longer the speech of the people. The young Italian language was everywhere spoken, but many generations passed before it found expression in writing. Like all growths of enduring fibre its development was slow, so late as the eleventh century; but few laymen, no matter how high their rank, were able to sign their names. Instruments of writing were signed with the mark of the cross.

But the sixth century had not closed before the leaven of deterioration began to work in the monasteries. Their constantly increasing wealth engendered idleness, and idleness is ever the fruitful mother of useless luxury and of vice. The monasteries continued to degenerate until their industry and frugality, their simplicity and purity were well-nigh lost. But as of old there were a faithful few who did not bow the knee to Baal.

Benedict of Nursia founded a new order of monks upon a higher moral basis, though his rule of life was less austere than that of existing orders. St. Benedict was educated in Rome, but in his early manhood he became disgusted with the dissipations of the schools and of the city, and to escape the general contamination he withdrew for a time not only from Rome but from the world to the solitude of hermit life. Subsequently he began his great work of monastic reformation. It is recorded of St. Benedict that late in his life he converted a body of pagan mountaineers and turned their temple into a monastery, and spent in that monastery the remainder of his days.

The impetus given by the work of St. Benedict re-aroused a wide-spread missionary spirit. Through the earnest labors of Augustine and his monks all Saxon Britain had professed Christianity before the close of the seventh century. Anterior to the Saxon conquest the Celtic church of Britain was an important church; so early as the fifth century she had sent missionaries into Gaul and Belgium. But the Saxon conquerors were heathen, and had broken up and partially detroyed the native church, but still to some extent, the Celtic church held its own. And after the establishment of the Roman church in the British isles the Celtic church still made its influence felt as a distinct church, until the conference of Whitby, when the two churches agreed to set aside minor differences and become one, and as one church labor for the Saxon tribes of Britain and for the whole population of the British isles, and also for the peoples of the continent. A British Benedictine monk, Winifred, went over to the continent and among the Frieslanders, Hessians and other Germanic tribes labored so long and successfully that he is known to history as St. Boniface, the Apostle of Germany.

The Venerable Bede was a native Englishman, born in the county of Durham. He was the most eminent scholar and writer of his age; he is called the father of English history. Bede was born about A. D. 673, and when about seven years old he was given by his parents in charge to the Abbot of the Wearmouth and Jarrow monastery, to be, like Samuel, brought up in the house of the Lord. Referring to the days of his youth the Venerable Bede writes, "I always took delight in learning, in teaching, and in writing. In the nineteenth year of my age I received deacon's orders, in the thirtieth I was ordained priest." His fame as a scholar and a teacher was known throughout all western Europe, and attracted hundreds of students to the monastic school of Jarrow.

His industry was untiring. He was the officiating priest, the preacher, the teacher, the careful student, and writer. He wrote on many subjects and wrote both in prose and poetry. His best known, and perhaps his greatest work, is his Ecclesiastical History; he brought it down to 731, four years before his death. Bede wrote in Latin. King Alfred translated Bede's history into Anglo-Saxon.

A letter has been preserved, written by his pupil, Cuthbert, which gives a touching picture of his death. Cuthbert says, "Though suffering much, and drawing his breath with pain, he conversed with his pupils, and at times sang psalms, and was full of thanksgiving and rejoicing." To his last hour he was translating, by dictation, into Anglo-Saxon the gospel according to St. John. To his pupil scribe he said, "Write fast, I shall not be with you much longer." The last word was translated and written down only some half hour before his saintly spirit left its well-worn tenement of clay.

The learning and the writings of the Venerable Bede scarcely justify the assertion of Dr. Hallam, that the seventh century was the nadir of the human mind. Though Bede lived into the eighth century, thirty-five years, and his greatest work was done in the eighth century, yet the workman was made ready for his work in the seventh century. But in general application Dr. Hallam is certainly right as when he says, "The advance movement of the human mind began with Charlemagne in the next century."

The civil and religious development of western Europe were not separate movements, developing on parallel lines. They were the two phases of the united action of mental and spiritual forces, quickened by the influence of Christianity. The influence of Christianity may be as clearly seen in the improved conditions of life, as in the growth of the church.

It was the harmonizing and civilizing influence of the Christian religion, which slowly and often under the burden of monstrous error brought western Europe from the darkness of the fifth century to the light and liberty of the sixteenth. And to appreciate fairly the breadth and the depth of the influence of Christianity it is necessary to consider together the civil and religious growth of the country.

The introduction of Christianity among the Germanic peoples was the sowing of the seed which produced the fruit that ripened into such men as Karl the Great (Charlemagne) and Alfred the Great, epoch making men. These two men stand at the head of the great army of human progression, which made western Europe the centre of the highest civilization of the world. Charlemagne, the leader of the advance guard, was the greatest man of his age; he was great as chieftain and warrior, great as statesman and scholar, and as monarch he was wise. He was a liberal patron of learning, and he gathered about him the best scholars of the time. He encouraged all branches of industry; he gave new life to commerce by the great roads he constructed; by means of a great road he opened up the country from the Elbe to the Danube, and after a time he continued the same road on to the Black sea. And a still greater undertaking was the road from the Mediterranean to the North sea.

He gave special attention to the education of his people; for his own children and those of the nobles he established the Palatine school, in which the pupils were to be instructed by the best masters in what were then known as the seven liberal arts, or branches of learning; and he inaugurated a system of free schools for the general good of his people.

The borders of his empire were often harassed by the Saxons, a fierce, brave people, who had defied the Roman eagles. Charlemagne determined to subdue and to convert them; he found it a difficult task, and when, after twelve years, he succeeded in subduing them and inducing them to accept Christianity, it was accomplished more through his liberality than by the force of his arms. To make sure of them he established schools in various parts of their country and built a number of monasteries.

In his own age, and in many succeeding ages, the chief fame of Charlemagne was that of the conquering hero, the resistless monarch; but in these later years his greatness is seen from a more humane point of view, as the promoter of civilization and the friend of education. He is said to have written the first German grammar.

The eighth century was one of great aggrandizement to the church. Charlemagne, as Emperor of the west, possessed in Rome supreme imperial power, but to the pope he granted authority over the city of Rome and the adjacent territory, which was afterward known as the states of the church, and over these the pope ruled with sovereign power. Many nobles gave their castles to the church, and princes gave royal domains; and some of the kings transferred cities and whole provinces to monasteries and to bishops. Bishops became sovereign lords, they administered civil law, and marched to war at the head of their armies. And the pope made a long stride toward temporal power.

Louis the Meek, the son and successor of Charlemagne, was equally zealous for the propagation of Christianity among the heathen. During his reign the Danes, Swedes and other northern tribes were partially converted to the Christian religion. At the same time by zealous and devout monks Christianity was preached to the Slavonian tribes. Charles the Bold, like his illustrious grandfather, was the patron of learning; he enlarged and improved the Palatine school, and he greatly increased the number and improved the condition of the free schools of his empire.

CHAPTER XII.
THE BRITISH ISLES.

IN the ninth century the greatest men are from the isles of Britain. John Erigena Scotus, a native of Ireland, stands pre-eminent as a scholar and as a Christian philosopher. The sum and substance of his great exposition of Christian philosophy consists in his conclusive argument that the chief aim of the whole Christian system is to bring the minds and hearts of men into harmony with the divine will through holiness of life, and holiness is only to be attained by continuous and close communion with God, through our Lord Jesus Christ.

In the ninth century Alfred of England, stands unequaled as warrior and statesman, as scholarly and Christian king. Alfred was the rescuer of his country, the victorious champion of Christianity against the pagans, as Saxon chroniclers term the Danes.

The pagan Danes possessed superior prowess in war; they had nearly harassed the warlike spirit out of the Anglo-Saxons, and then they taunted them with having become a race of women under the influence of their new religion.

Continuous defeats had so disheartened the people that it was almost impossible to raise an army and bring it into action at the time when the crown was placed on young Alfred's head. The young king was brave, and full of enthusiasm for his country and for his religion, but he found it a most difficult task to enkindle enthusiasm in the hearts of his discouraged and almost starving people. The supineness of his people and the loss of his stronghold Chippenham, reduced the young king to sad straits, as related by his friend and biographer, Asser, bishop of Sherborn. But after many efforts he succeeded in arousing their dormant courage and patriotism so far that he was enabled to raise an army and march at their head to battle. The army of the enemy far outnumbered them, but Alfred gained a decisive victory. This victory put heart into the Saxons. Numbers readily enlisted under the royal banner and gladly followed their brave young king, who led them on from victory to victory, driving the invaders before him as far as his northeastern border; there he suffered them to remain under their own laws, but subject to him as their king. Alfred's clemency was also sagacious statesmanship; the Danes, as his subjects, settled on his northeastern border were a bulwark against further Danish invasion.

King Alfred restored the dismantled fortresses and built new ones, especially along the coast.

To prevent the army and people from being again reduced to a state of destitution and partial starvation Alfred would only permit one-half of the able bodied men of his kingdom to enter the army; the other half were to engage in industrial pursuits, of which the chief was farming.

The Danes had partially destroyed many cities, and had demolished the monasteries and their libraries. Alfred restored the cities, rebuilt the monasteries, and refilled their libraries. He also invited to England skilled workmen in the various mechanical arts from all the countries of Europe. King Alfred laid the foundation of English commerce, and of English liberty. Before his time public justice could only be sought in the local courts of earls and bishops. Alfred appointed special judges, who were sworn to decide fairly and uprightly, and he ordered that the accused be tried by twelve of his compeers.

To Alfred the Great, England and America owe the right of trial by jury. And he is the first of the rulers of the world who made the sacredness of human life the basis of advancing civilization. He repealed the ancient law of composition for blood by payment of money to the survivors, and he placed all possible safeguards around human life and liberty.

His biblical preface to the Code of Law concludes with the law of Christ, "Whatsoever ye would that men should do unto you, do ye even so to them." His Code of Law began with the Ten Commandments, which were followed by extracts from the Mosaic law, bearing on murder and other crimes, and on the relations between masters and servants. And King Alfred opened commercial relations with the east by sending an embassy to the traditional church of St. Thomas in India.

Alfred the Great was not only a patriot, statesman and wise king, he was also a scholar and an inventor; he found it necessary, in order to prevent waste of his precious time, to devise some means by which he could methodically apportion his evening hours to his varied work. This led to his invention of the famous candle clock, but their houses were so rudely built that the candle clock was liable to be blown out by any passing blast of wind. In this exigency the king set himself to the task of overcoming so serious a difficulty, and he succeeded; the further invention of the transparent horn lantern made his candle clock secure in house or tent.

That Alfred founded a school in the royal city of Oxford has been satisfactorily proven: that he laid the foundations of University college has been ratified by the Court of King's Bench, though there are historical critics who protest against such foundation.

It is claimed by some writers that Alfred the

THE BRITISH ISLES. 81

Great translated the whole Bible into Anglo-Saxon, but no positive proof can be adduced that he translated any other portion than the book of Psalms. For the use of the clergy of his kingdom and for the general good of his people he translated "The Pastoral Care" of Gregory the Great, and to this excellent book he added other works translated from early Christian authors; but he did not confine himself to religious works, he translated the general history of Orosius, and a geographical description of Germany, and he wrote down a book of explorations on the coasts of the Baltic, and of the North seas.

"Othere, the old sea captain,
 Who dwelt in Helgoland,
To King Alfred, the Lover of truth,
 Brought a snow-white walrus tooth,
 Which he held in his brown right hand.

And Alfred, king of the Saxons,
 Had a book upon his knees,
And wrote down the wondrous tale
Of him who was first to sail
 Into the Arctic seas.

And to the king of the Saxons,
 In witness of the truth,
Raising his noble head,
He stretched his brown hand, and said,
 Behold this walrus tooth."

The foundations laid by Alfred the Great have proven to be enduring foundations. He laid not only the foundation of University college, but he laid the foundation of the political liberty of England, and also of her literary glory.

When the great Alfred found that the days of the years of his life were numbered, in Christian resignation he wrote, "I can truly say that so long as I have lived I have striven to live worthily, and to leave my memory to my people, and to my descendants in good works." Let the memory of Alfred the Great be kept green in the hearts of all English speaking people.

The kingdom rescued and united by the courage and wisdom of Alfred the Great, has continued from that time to this present time a political unity unbroken, whether ruled by Saxon or Norman, whether governed as commonwealth or kingdom.

CHAPTER XIII.

THE CRUSADES.

AFTER the death of Charlemagne and of his immediate descendants the empire he founded fell to pieces. France, the most important part of the empire, was not able to preserve her political unity, her kings could not hold their authority against the great vassals who claimed their fiefs as patrimonial sovereignties, and exercised in their dominions sovereign rights; they refused all tribute, save military duty. The greatest of these vassals, the Dukes of Burgundy, maintained a state equal to that of the kings of France, until that far-seeing, crafty and most unscrupulous of French kings, Louis XI., released himself and his successors from their overweening power, and laid the foundation of a despotism which culminated under Louis XIV.

On the continent commerce developed at an earlier date than it did in England; in the south of France and in Spain there was trade in money as early as the sixth century. The trade for several centuries was chiefly in the hands of Jews, who traded to such advantage that they grew rich in money and in landed estates, and they held important civil offices, but the jealousy of native traders, combined with religious fanaticism, raised against them a bitter persecution; they were deprived of their privileges, and their property was taken from them.

The further development of industry and commerce was seriously retarded by those martial pilgrimages, known as the crusades. The injuries and insults heaped upon Christians living in Jerusalem, and upon palmers, and all other Christians going on pilgrimages to the holy city, led Pope Sylvester II., near the close of the tenth century, to address a letter to the church universal in behalf of the church at Jerusalem; he specially impressed upon the Christians of Europe the duty of aiding the suffering church at Jerusalem. But Europe did not respond to the appeal. Nor was Pope Gregory VII. more successful in his proposed war against the Mohammedans, but it is most probable that Gregory VII. was not really anxious for the war,—it would have interfered with his diplomatic schemes at home. Gregory VII. was an intrepid and daring man, sagacious and of superior talents, and during his whole life he schemed and labored to increase the opulence and enlarge the jurisdiction of the See of Rome; and he succeeded in making kings and princes tributary to the Pope of Rome as the vicegerent of Christ.

Not until near the close of the eleventh century did the idea of the holy war become an actual thing, and then not through pope or potentate, but through Peter, the hermit of Picardy. Peter the Hermit went on a pilgrimage to Jerusalem, and beholding the cruel treatment to which Christians were subjected, his spirit burned within him, and staff in hand he returned to lay the case before the pope, Urban II. But the pope was not then minded to move in the matter, but Peter the Hermit was not thus to be silenced. He traveled on foot over Europe, and by his fervent zeal and eloquence he aroused the enthusiasm of princes and of people to proclaim a holy war for the recovery of the sepulchre of Christ from the infidel.

The general enthusiasm was so thoroughly aroused that he was regarded as one divinely inspired, and his utterances were received as the commandments of God. So intense was the public excitement that the pope found it necessary to assemble a council and recommend the war, which was called the Crusade, because the purpose was to rescue the sepulchre of Christ from its enemies, and all who engaged in the war were required to wear the emblem of the cross.

All classes of people flocked in multitudes to the standard of the Cross; priests left their parishes, monks their monasteries, women and children their homes, to swell the concourse, believing that to engage in the crusade was to merit heaven, and to die in it was to win the immortal crown of the martyr.

That army was a mighty host, but comparatively few of them returned to tell of the recovery of the Holy Sepulchre and of the newly established Christian kingdom of Jerusalem, of which Godfrey of Bouillon was made king.

In less than fifty years the eastern conquests, to gain which so large a host had perished, were so harassed by the enemy that it was found necessary to undertake another crusade for their relief. Near the middle of the twelfth century the Emperor, Conrad II., and Louis VII., of France, started on the second crusade with one hundred and forty thousand cavalry. Without accomplishing its purpose that vast army wasted away.

Later in the century, 1187, the great Saracen Saladin besieged Jerusalem and took the city. The fall of Jerusalem, the destruction of the Christian kingdom, startled and aroused all Europe; armies for the third and most celebrated crusade were raised. The Emperor, Frederic Barbarossa, Philip Augustus of France, and Richard the Lion Hearted of England, assembled their armies at Nicæ in Asia Minor, and along the march from that place to Jerusalem their lances carried everything before them.

History and romance have combined to weave a charm about the leading men, and the exploits of the third and most famous crusade, though it actually accomplished but little. Subsequently other crusades were undertaken, they were of no great magnitude, and none of them reached the Holy Land.

The early force of the crusade fever well nigh destroyed the industries and trade of the countries of Europe, but in the end both manufactures and trade were benefited; the commercial prosperity of the Italian republics may be dated from the crusades. The art of silk manufacture was brought from the east, the first silk factory was established at Palermo, and silk soon became the staple manufacture of the northern states of Italy. Notwithstanding the general excitement created by the crusades, and the loss to Europe of large armies of men, there can be traced through the twelfth century a tolerably steady material and intellectual improvement. The twelfth, thirteenth and fourteenth centuries have been aptly termed "light bearing centuries." Under their gradually increasing light lay the long and crooked path which led on to the Renaissance, or Revival of Learning, in the fifteenth century, and to the Reformation, or Revival of Religion in the sixteenth.

The thirteenth was an eventful century in the ecclesiastical world, and it was also a most important century in the political development of Europe. As far back as the eleventh century no small number among the bishops strove after princely expenditure, and they carried their extravagance so far that their large revenues were not sufficient to defray their expenses, and they consequently resorted to unholy means of raising money. They distributed among the people papers of remittance for any penalties that had been imposed on them within a specified limit of-time. The papers of remittance were subsequently called *indulgences*, and the traffic in them was carried to such an extent that the papal power took the matter in hand. The pope limited the power of the bishops in the matter, but he enlarged the scope of the indulgences by giving plenary remission of all penalties in this life, and some of the indulgences extended the remission to the life beyond the grave. The assumption of papal power was such that Pope Boniface VIII., in the thirteenth century, did not hesitate to declare that the pope's power was absolute; as the vicar of Christ he held in his hands all power in church and state, and none had a right to question his edicts. And Christianity was required to be so taught as to make it support these arrogant claims.

The frugal, laborious, simple hearted monks had disappeared, monasteries had become the sumptuous homes of lazy, vicious men. But strenuous efforts were made by those who still held the purity and simplicity of the faith as it is in Christ to reform both monks and monasteries. The most active of the reformers banded themselves into an order known as the Order of Mendicant Monks. These monks rejected all permanent possessions and revenues. But alas! the time came when these reformers, bloated with the greed of rank and lust of power, sank into a degeneracy not exceeded by that which they came to reform.

But when, in the thirteenth century, they were first established in Europe, they were zealous of good works, and fearless preachers of the simple gospel; they boldly reproached the church for her excess of wealth, and the clergy for the unholiness of their lives. They spread themselves over all Europe as missionaries and teachers; they were undaunted by hardships, and unmoved by the attractions of wealth, or by worldly preferments. At the same time they were implicit believers in the supreme power of the pope, and were devout in their loyalty to the successor of St. Peter. And the popes were not slow to perceive the advantage to be gained through the adherence of this widespread and popular order.

Successive popes granted to the Mendicant Orders full liberty to found churches and schools throughout the length and breadth of the church.

The voluntary poverty and earnest piety of the Mendicants called forth general enthusiasm and reverence; their reputation for sanctity drew eager crowds to their churches to drink in their teachings and to receive the sacraments from their hands. Persons of highest rank were eager to become members of the Mendicant Order. Some while in health, others when they felt their end to be approaching, begged to be admitted to the order, believing that to become a Mendicant was to secure special favor from God in this world, and in the world to come.

Inflated with papal privileges and popular favor, combined with the weakness of human nature, the Mendicants lost their first estate, and by transgression fell into pride, arrogance and cruelty. They filled the chief places in church and state, their counsel guided matters ecclesiastical and political.

They were merciless against all forms of what they termed heresy. They hunted to the death all persons who were suspected of disloyalty to the See of Rome, and tracked them with inquisitive pursuit to their homes, which could no longer afford them safety.

Papal legates were sent to hunt out the Waldenses and Albigenses, Christian sects which rejected the arrogant claims of the papacy, and lived nearer to the simplicity of primitive Christianity. The Mendicants eagerly joined the papal legates and pushed to the front in the terrible army of persecutors. Finding neither promises nor threats could induce these brave Christians to acknowledge the pope as the supreme earthly head of the church they subjected them to tortures too fearful to describe. This inquisition for blood gave rise to that terrible tribunal, The Court of the Inquisition, a blot on the papal church, a blot on humanity.

The religious, civil and intellectual growth in Europe during the thirteenth and fourteenth centuries under the most adverse conditions is a most remarkable proof of the force of the divine fiat, Go Forward, spoken not to the Israelites only, but to the soul of man, of every race, and for all time.

The contest for sovereign power between popes and emperors was to some extent paralyzing to the forces working out the civilization of western Europe, but notwithstanding all drawbacks humanity moved forward.

CHAPTER XIV.

CIVIL PROSPECTS BRIGHTEN.

EARLY in the fourteenth century Pope Clement V., who was a Frenchman, was induced by the king of France to transfer the papal court from Rome to Avignon, a city in France; and the papal court was held in Avignon for a period of seventy years. Affairs in Rome went from bad to worse during that time. The conviction on the minds of the papal party in the ancient city was that the salvation of the city depended on the restoration of the papal court to Rome. Near the middle of the century a deputation was sent to Avignon to beseech the pope, Clement VI., to return to Rome. Rienzi, the eloquent Roman, was sent with this deputation as special pleader or orator, but neither his eloquence nor the prayers of the deputation could effect the desired purpose. The disappointed deputation returned to Rome, but Rienzi remained at Avignon until the following year. He then returned to Rome filled with ideas of reform, and he sought to win over the magistrates to his views, but in vain; reform was impossible without revolution. To inaugurate the needed revolutionary movement he induced the papal legate and a hundred cavalryman to act in concert with him. He then ordered a general gathering of the citizens; in response to the call a large multitude assembled, and when brought to order Rienzi proclaimed to them a formulated code of law for the better government of the state. This was received with enthusiastic and unanimous approval, and the people were eager to make Rienzi dictator, and to invest him at once with the title. He accepted the rulership, but declined the aristocratic title of dictator; he preferred, according to the democratic usage of ancient Rome, to be known as Tribune of the People.

A graphic picture of Rienzi and his times is to be found in Bulwer's "Rienzi, or the Last of the Tribunes."

Later in the fourteenth century the untiring efforts of the papal party were crowned with success. In 1376 Pope Gregory XI., in order to recover the cities and territories which had been wrested from the patrimony of St. Peter, and to restore tranquillity to Italy, removed the papal court back to Rome. The return was greeted with tumultuous acclamations of delight, not only in Rome, but throughout Italy.

After the death of Gregory XI. the unity of the Romish church as existing under one head came to an end. For the next fifty years the church had two, and sometimes three popes, each plotting against the other, and each hurling at the other maledictions and excommunications. The wars between the papal factions were severe drawbacks to the prosperity of the country, and to a large extent they extinguished all sense of spiritual religion.

Conscientious men, believers in the supremacy of the pope as the one sole successor of St. Peter, the Vicar of Christ, men who were not partisans in the strife, were sorely perplexed as to what they should believe.

Among the higher clergy a large number ceased to care even for the appearance of godliness. "Why should we care?" their conduct seemed to ask, "when the headship of the church is claimed by men who are at open war, and are not choice in their methods of warfare?" This dreadful condition of affairs after it was settled did not apparently injure the supremacy of the pope, but it was actually an undermining influence from which the papal power never afterward entirely recovered. But from the civil and intellectual points of view the prospect in Europe is brighter than from the ecclesiastical and religious.

From the time the Emperor, Henry V., admitted artisans to the privileges of free burghers, German cities grew more and more prosperous, their lack of maritime advantages was measurably compensated by the steady industry and frugality of the citizens. Near the middle of the thirteenth century the four chief cities, Lubec, Hamburg, Bremen and Dantzic, with other less important cities, formed the famous commercial confederation known as the Hanseatic League. In England the traders of the Hanseatic League were favored above all others, because England found in the cities on the Baltic sea an important market for her exports. Her vessels at that time seldom ventured so far from home as the Mediterranean, nor did French and Italian vessels often attempt the long and perilous voyage to the rough northern seas. Edward III. was so deeply interested in the commercial development of his country that he introduced into England the manufacture of fine woolen goods, and offered to the oppressed manufacturers of Flanders a safe home in England. And the king's avowed interest in commerce caused the occupation of merchant to become an honored calling in England. Under the long and prosperous reign of Edward III. the leading objects of Parliament were the establishing of commerce on a solid foundation and the securing of political liberty. But thereafter the maritime relations of the countries of Europe were completely revolutionized by the rediscovery of the mariner's compass; henceforth all sea-coast towns or cities became neighbors.

The merchants of the south of France, and of Lombardy, during the thirteenth century had been in the habit of remitting money by bills of exchange, charging profit on loans. After the mariner's compass came into use, this mode of exchange grew to such proportions that a bank of deposit for mercantile accommodation was established at Barcelona in the first year of the fifteenth century. About this time the Spanish Arabs were a leading people in Europe, both in industry and in learning. They were so liberal in their interpretations of the Koran that its prohibitions did not prevent them from excelling in music, poetry and romance. To the Spanish Arabs Europe is indebted for Algebra, Geometry, and our nine graceful figures, and also for our decimal system of notation. The Arabs of Spain gave special attention to agriculture, both practically and as an art, and they sacredly observed their Moslem adage, "Who so planteth trees and tilleth the ground to make it bring forth fruit for man and beast, shall have it reckoned to him in heaven."

All through the long Arab occupation of Spain the native Spaniards held three small kingdoms in the northern mountains, and continued to keep up a harassing warfare against the conquerors, and about the middle of the thirteenth century they achieved a partial conquest. They retook three of the principal cities, pulled down the crescent and replanted the cross, though it was not until near the close of the fifteenth century that the power of the Arabs was entirely broken up, and they were driven out of Spain.

The Palatine school at Paris had grown into the foremost school in Europe, and was the first to enlarge its curriculum so as to embrace the whole circle then known of the arts and sciences, and it was therefore the first school in Europe to become an university. But institutions of learning in other countries were not slow in following the lead of Paris. Universities were soon to be found in all the great countries of Europe.

Though the university courses embraced all the known arts and sciences, the students devoted themselves chiefly, during the thirteenth century, to philosophy and to canon and civil law; and the learned doctors wrote and wrangled about Realism and Nominalism and theological subtleties, until they must have bewildered themselves, as they have ever since bewildered their readers. But even then a bright star shone through the intellectual haze. Roger Bacon turned from scholasticism and abstruse unsatisfying subtleties to seek a knowledge of nature by means of actual experiment. But alas! Friar Bacon was ahead of his age, and his methods were beyond the comprehension of his fellows. He was exiled from his native England, and in France he had to undergo ten years of imprisonment.

To the prevailing influence of the scholasticism of the thirteenth century may be attributed the decline from the classical literature of the twelfth century, but it was fortunate from the fact that the dearth of classical literature called forth native literatures.

All literatures have found their first expression in poetry. During the thirteenth century many native Italian poets helped to mould their mother tongue into her admirable musical proportions, over which in the fourteenth century, Petrarch had such perfect command. He was the popular poet of his day, but his more enduring fame is as the inaugurator of the intellectual freedom of Europe. He had an impassioned love of ancient culture, and was zealous in restoring it. The renown of Petrarch incited Boccaccio to the study of classic authors, and that study led him to devote himself to the work of restoration.

Dante is called the father of Italian poetry, not because he was the first to write in the Italian tongue, but because he was, and is, the *great poet* of Italy.

CHAPTER XV.

Light Bearing Centuries.

In Germany the lyric poets, or minnesingers, were numerous from the twelfth to the fifteenth century. Of German epics of that period the Helden Buch and the Nibelungen Lied are the most celebrated. These poems contain some graphic pictures of heroism and of tragedy. And in Germany were the Meister-singers, whose productions were serious and moral, but were lacking in the power of the greater epics, and in the lightness and grace of the minnesingers.

France was filled with the song of the Trouveurs and Troubadours; the Romaunt du Rose of De Loris aided in developing and fashioning the genius of Chaucer, who also caught from across the channel the "Sweet Iambic," which still remains a favorite measure in English poetry.

Our direct, yet flexible and elegant English, was comparatively late in its application to literature. Early in the fourteenth century several metrical romances were translated from the French. Later in that century the first original book was written in the English language, as distinguished from the Anglo-Saxon. It was entitled "Piers Plowman's Vision." The book is a metrical satire upon the clergy, and is a spirited portraiture of the times, but the measure is uncouth. The first original prose work written and published in English, about the middle of the fourteenth century, was a book of travels by Sir John Mandeville. Honor to Sir John, father of English prose, though he apologized for writing in so rude a tongue.

Later Chaucer wrote his "Canterbury Tales," poems full of vivacity, good feeling and keen observation, and they show a quick sense of the ludicrous side of life, but are rather lacking in dignity. Chaucer is justly ranked among the great poets of the middle ages. Near about the same time John Wycliffe translated the Bible into English.

The great advance made in learning during the fourteenth century and the first half of the fifteenth, justify the claim made for that hundred and fifty years of being the "Herald of the Renaissance, a herald whose armor is bright with auroral gleams, bright with the rosy light of morning that ushers in the day." Not only is the herald bright with morning's rosy light, but he flashes his light on the portal of that morning, illuminating three men who stand at that portal; three men, Dante, Petrarch, and Chaucer, about whose brows the "rosy light" condenses into an enduring halo; three men whom

"we must measure as the Cretan sage
Measured the pyramids of ages past.
By the far reaching shadows which they cast."

PART III.

CHAPTER XVI.
REVIVAL OF LEARNING.

ALL important epochs which have marked the history of the world have grown out of antecedent causes, and their lines of demarkation are so interwoven with the past on the one hand and with the future on the other, that it is impossible to determine definitely the limits of any historical epoch.

That remarkable outburst of intellectual activity which separates Modern Times from the Middle Ages, and yet unites them in historic continuity, may, in a general way, be reckoned as reaching from the fall of the Greek empire, A. D. 1453, to the sack of Rome in 1527. But for a century or more previous to the fall of the Greek empire monasteries, schools and individuals had been accumulating manuscripts, coins and medals, and otherwise had been striving to reinstate learning. But the general diffusion of Greek literature, science and art brought about by the exodus of learned men from Constantinople, after the capture of the city by the Turks, was the immediate cause of the Renaissance or Revival of Letters.

The zeal and enthusiasm for the restoration of ancient learning in Italy was at fever heat, but in the countries to the north of her the enthusiasm kindled slowly. So late as 1661 Dr. Barrow, professor of Greek at Oxford, complains that no students attend the lectures on Greek. He says, "I sit alone as an attic owl driven out from the society of all other birds."

In Italy the enthusiastic zeal in intellectual pursuits, combined with church love, induced quite a number of her scholars to endeavor to harmonize Christianity and ancient philosophy. In an earlier age the pope and the clergy generally would have frowned upon the movement and have silenced the men who attempted it, but in that age both pope and clergy had to some extent caught the spirit of the classic past, and became leaders in the effort to unite ecclesiastical tradition and idealized paganism.

As far back as the eleventh century some few fearless Italian scholars had criticised accepted canons, and cited precedents of liberty in the early church. That free spirit, though often silenced and persecuted, lived on, vitalizing and expanding the new movement by spreading the old Hellenic faith in the greatness of the human intellect. That old faith re-awakened confidence in human ability, and is the link which connects ancient and modern history.

Among the gifted Italian scholars who labored with untiring zeal for the revival, or new birth of learning, Petrarch may be fairly regarded as the chief pioneer. He was the first to seek coins, medals and inscriptions as sources of accurate historical information, and he was the first to advocate public libraries. His constant warfare against the narrowness of scholastic theology, and against whatever obstructed the free activity of the intellect entitle him not only to the rank of chief pioneer, but to the higher position of father of the Italian Renaissance.

Petrarch was ably seconded by Boccaccio. Boccaccio's conception of life as a blessing to be enjoyed, not an evil to be lamented, and his delight in the human body, which he taught should be admired and cared for, not despised and scourged as hermits and monks had taught, were teachings which came as an inspiration to artists, leading them to study the human form divine, and to paint beautiful, life-like pictures, instead of continuing to copy the uncouth figures of saints that had been blessed by the church and were reverenced by the people.

But that unexampled intellectual activity was not confined to reintroducing classic literature and to regenerating art. It broke the swaddling bands of scholasticism, by which science had been well nigh suffocated, and science regaining new life-breath gave to the world Copernicus, father of modern astronomy.

Copernicus made a careful study of the whole reach of mathematical and astronomical science then known to the world, and afterward made a careful comparison of the various astronomical schemes that had been set forth in different ages, including the accepted Ptolemaic system. The comparison led him to adopt and confirm the scheme of Pythagoras as the only one capable of explaining planetary motions with a simplicity which in itself is a presumption of truth.

After years of preparatory labor he began his great work, which was completed about the year 1530.

Copernicus set forth his theory as a hypothesis; he may have chosen this form as a protection against the blind, bigoted prejudice of his age, an age in which men tenaciously held as religious truth the belief that the earth was the fixed centre of creation, around which sun, moon and stars were made only to revolve, to light, to warm, to make fruitful.

Through the whole history of our race it has ever proved a difficult task to uproot deep seated prejudices, especially so when they assume a religious character. It would have been a useless risk in Copernicus, and he may not have felt himself prepared to set forth his profound theory in a positive form.

In that age to teach that the earth is a planet, a member of a system of planets, all moving with a double motion around their central sun, was setting forth a sublime truth which it had never entered the mind of man to conceive. In a later age for declaring this wonderful truth Galileo was stretched on the rack of the inquisition.

The book of Copernicus was first published by his disciple, Rhæticus, at Nuremberg, in 1540. Three years later Copernicus wrote a dedication to the pope, Paul III., and with the dedication he himself republished the work. The first copy was brought to him as he lay on his death-bed; with his dying hand he touched the book, which was to be the beacon light signalling men away from the complex Ptolemaic to the Copernican system, so sublime in its simplicity, sublime in its reach of thought, in its awe-inspiring conception of systems of starry worlds filling the infinitude of space.

Although the gifted men who rounded out the great theory of Copernicus belong to the beginning of modern times, yet the names of Kepler, Galileo, Tycho Brahe and Grassi should ever be associated with the name of Copernicus. The refracting telescope for astronomical purposes was one of the great inventions of Galileo.

Among the Saracens the telescope had been long in use, but was unknown to Europeans until the middle of the thirteenth century, when it was introduced by Roger Bacon.

Later, by some century or more, the mariner's compass was invented by Flavio of Naples. The Chinese claim the compass as an ancient invention of theirs. They date it as far back as 2634 years before the Christian era. They prove from their national annals that the instrument was not only used in their country, but that most of the countries of the east used their invention to guide the course of their ships and of their caravans across the deserts long anterior to the time of Christ.

Without questioning the correctness of their claim it is safe to state that it scarcely comes within the scope of probability that the Chinese compass was ever known in Europe previous to Flavio's invention, which in some points differed essentially from that of the Chinese, being suited to a different order of civilization.

Without the aid of the mariner's compass Columbus could not have carried out his bold purpose of sailing far to the westward across the stormy Atlantic in order to find a direct ocean path to India, and instead to find a new world, the greatest achievement of the Middle Ages. And here again that remarkable people, the Chinese, claim a long anterior discovery; they claim that a party of their Buddhist monks voyaged across the Pacific ocean and discovered the country on the Pacific coast as early as A. D. 432, and in 464 a second expedition came to the country, and on their return the account of their voyage and discovery was entered in the Chinese Year Book. But their discoveries, as those of the Norsemen, and of the traditional discoveries of the Welsh, were of no value to the world. Columbus remains the great discoverer.

But to the old Saxon love of liberty, law and order brought over from freedom-loving England is to be ascribed the true greatness of the hemisphere which Columbus added to the map of the world.

The Teuton love of liberty transplanted in America struck deep root, and brought forth a vigorous growth of new activities and new ideas, which have quickened the pulse of the world, and are developing on both sides of the Atlantic a higher civilization, a broader humanity, and a simpler, purer Christianity.

Ever thus through conditions suited to their

growth and strength God has led and still leads the children of men onward to the fulfillment of His own great purpose.

He stayed the conquering Turks when, flushed with the pride of conquest, they threatened the overthrow of southern Europe, and made the friends of learning tremble with anxious fear lest the Moslem should destroy the young culture in the bud and reduce Europe to a state of darkness deeper than that which followed the conquests of the Goths and vandals. But in the providence of God Europe was saved from the library-destroying people; scholars took heart again and turned to their work with renewed assiduity, and the fertile brains of inventors labored in travail, until they brought to birth the great invention of the world, the Art of Printing.

This most important invention came at a critical juncture, though following in direct line of succession the invention of paper and the rebirth of learning. It came to make that learning a sure and permanent blessing; it came to scatter with liberal hand the seeds of culture broadcast over the world.

Stamping or printing from carved blocks of wood had been done from a high antiquity in China. In Europe the first efforts towards printing were made in Holland. In the early part of the fourteenth century the Hollanders carved raised figures of saints on blocks of wood, and carved words below the figures. Subsequently blocks of wood were cut into tablets and the tablets were filled with carved writing; they were called block books. Some few are still extant. Such was the humble beginning of the world renewing art.

Those honored Germans, Guttenburg, Fust and Schaeffer, were the fathers of the great art which they gradually perfected without the aid of the learned Italian scholars, who were eagerly seeking, but slowly transcribing, the higher branches of learning.

The first known book issued from the press of Guttenburg, Fust and Schaeffer is the Mazarin Bible, dated 1450. It is called the Mazarin Bible because it was found in the library of Cardinal Mazarin.

In various cities of Germany, Holland and France printing presses were established, and all the chief cities of Italy soon followed their example, and in those monasteries which were rich in manuscripts printing presses were set up. In England William Caxton established the printing press in the year 1472, twenty years before Columbus started on his world discovering voyage.

In 1474 printing presses were introduced into Spain. The art of printing so perfectly met the need of the time that the fathers of the invention and their coadjutors toiled night and day at their presses to meet the demand. The Bible was carefully revised, many interpolations being cast out,—and scholars by the score were employed on the classics to ascertain the correct rendering of sentences, and to prepare generally for the press.

CHAPTER XVII.

SIR THOMAS MORE—ERASMUS.

THE interest in preserving and disseminating classic culture was so absorbing that it repressed original production. The first important original work of the Renaissance comes from England, Sir Thomas More's "Utopia." Some writers claim that the work is based on the Republic of Plato; while to some extent the claim may be just, yet the books are widely different. In "Utopia," the conception of human relations is purer, higher, and more delicate, and the sense of justice is finer. Sir Thomas More's insight into human nature, his perception of its better part and of its improvability, will secure to the book an abiding place in the literature of Europe and of America, though its name has been made a synonym for the impracticable. On its first publication the work had an extensive popularity.

The rank of foremost scholar of the Renaissance may be fairly accorded to Erasmus, who, "with trenchant blade unsparing," of irony and of invective, slew the giants of ignorance and of superstition which blocked up the path of learning. His "Praise of Folly," dedicated to his friend Sir Thomas More, is a poignant satire against princes and others in authority and against the mendicant monks. The popularity of the work was immense, eight hundred copies were sold as soon as it issued from the press.

Erasmus wrote chiefly on theology, though he by no means confined himself to that subject. His Colloquies profess to be written for the instruction and the amusement of youth, but both the instruction and amusement are at the expense of prevalent church errors in doctrine and usage. The eagerness to obtain the book was surprising; several thousands of copies were sold in less than a year. Dr. Hallam, in speaking of Erasmus, says: "He was the first conspicuous enemy of the ignorance and superstition of his time, the first restorer of Christian morality on a scriptural foundation, but he was averse to radical changes; his desire was to purify and preserve the unbroken communion of the Catholic church." But it was too late; that unbroken communion had been too sorely worsted by the anathematising contentions of contemporary popes, and by the general wickedness of the times. All the force of character and diplomatic skill of Nicholas V. were necessary to strengthen and confirm the power of the church, that she might be able, even for a while longer, to hold her power and communion unbroken.

When Nicholas V. was elected to the papacy in 1447, while no opposition was made to the spiritual authority of the pope, a conspiracy was formed to arouse republican enthusiasm, and prevent the pope from attempting to seize the reins of political power. But the times were not ripe for the successful carrying out of the purpose of the conspirators.

Nicholas crushed the conspiracy, caused the leaders to be arrested, and the chief movers to be put to death; he subdued the states of the church and brought them under the absolute temporal power of the papacy. Nicholas V. saw, from the course of events for more than a hundred years, that the spiritual despotism established by Gregory VII. no longer stood firm, no longer controlled the minds and consciences of men, and he resolved that the undefined or ill-defined temporal power of the papacy should become a clearly defined temporal despotism and serve as a strong support to the tottering spiritual despotism of the papacy.

Nicholas V. turned the Mausoleum of Hadrian into

a fortress, and spared no expense in rendering it impregnable; the bridge of St. Angelo he had defended by walls and strong outworks, so that, if occasion required, he could hold in command the city of Rome.

But, looking fairly over the turbulent and lawless condition of the times, the autocratic and martial course of Nicholas V. seems to have been a necessity. Absolute power in the hands of so able a man was, in such times, an unquestionable good to the people. He repressed turbulence and restored order, and he also restored the architectural grandeur of Rome and made her the centre of southern culture. He was the friend of the new learning, and he founded the Vatican library. His pontificate was brief, though full of activity; his death was lamented both by churchmen and scholars.

From the time of Nicholas V. the history of Italy, through many ages, is closely interwoven with the history of the papacy. During the half century following the death of Nicholas V. the papal changes have been compared "to the shifting scenes in a tragedy, in which one sees a passion for magnificence, an unblushing cynicism, a selfish cupidity and a savage ferocity of temper."

To study the life of Sextus IV. is to behold a tissue of all crimes. In the last quarter of the fifteenth century, for the extermination of Moors, Jews and heretics, he established the Court of the Inquisition in Spain. It makes the blood run cold to read of the tortures inflicted, and of the agonies of the thousands who were burned at the stake.

The Jewish population were utterly despoiled; they were robbed of their property and driven out of the country penniless. Hundreds perished from exposure and from famine before they could reach the sea coast, and to those who lived to gain the ships no friendly ports were open. Italy, blinded by a religious fanaticism as far removed from the religion of Christ as the nadir is from the zenith, closed her ports against the robbed and exiled Jews. Hundreds of the escaped remnants of that people perished from direst need in the harbors of Genoa and Naples; a fearful rebuke to those who claim that the former days were better than these latter days.

Under the pontificate of Innocent VIII. the country about Rome was overrun with brigands and murderers; assassinations were committed with impunity, even in the city of Rome. The pope determined that the patrimony of St. Peter should derive profit out of this lawless condition; so he established in Rome a bank for traffic in indulgences. Every crime had its pardon price. But his successor, Alexander VI., though he was an embodiment of the very genius of evil, was a sagacious man, of sound judgment, and profound diplomacy. He resolved to repress the banditti and establish order in Rome, and he carried out his resolution, but he held in his own hands the control of poisoners and assassins. The pope's favor was as dangerous as his frown. Alexander VI. often bestowed large wealth on men for whom he affected special fondness, and shortly after the bestowal of the bounty upon any rich man, cardinal or bishop, or layman, he would have that man adroitly poisoned, and confiscate his whole estate by appropriating it to the See of Rome, which meant himself.

The main objects of the life of Alexander VI. were the advancement of his family, and the consolidation of the temporal power of the papacy. His family name was Borgia; his son, Cæsar Borgia, was a famous general, and an infamous man,—a chip of the old block. The death of the pope was an untimely one, brought about by the machinations of the father and son against the life of another. Cardinal Adrian, the richest man in the college of Cardinals, was invited by the pope and his son to dine with them; the wine to be served to the Cardinal was prepared according to the most sure and subtle art of the poisoner.

The gracious invitation of the pontiff and his son was courteously accepted by the Cardinal, who secretly sent large bribes to the butler; in that case, the old adage proved true, "Like master, like man." The large bribe outweighed the butler's loyalty, pure wine was served in the Cardinal's cup, and the poisoned wine in the cups of the pope and his son; the pope fell a victim to his own crime.

It is related by a historian of the time, that "when the death of the pope was made public, all Rome was filled with indescribable gladness." The strong vital force of Cæsar Borgia enabled him to recover from the terrible poison. After some vicissitudes of fortune, he died a papal prisoner in Spain, under the pontificate of Julius II.

CHAPTER XVIII.
Dr. Martin Luther.

Leo X. was the youngest son of the great Lorenzo di Medici of Florence, and like his father, he was a scholar and a friend to learning. It is said of him that "he gave more study to classic authors and to a pure Latinity than he gave to the teachings of the church, or to the writings of the fathers."

Pope Leo X. possessed his father's urbanity but lacked his strength of character; and Pope Leo's religious convictions sat lightly on him. He did not hesitate to follow papal precedent in imposing on the superstitious credulity of his people, when he could thereby raise money to gratify his love of magnificent surroundings. Following the example of Julius II. he renewed the scandalous traffic in indulgences.

The renewal of that abominable traffic was the entering wedge, driven by the great hammer of the Reformation, which split in twain the visible church.

After the great Arian controversy in the fourth and fifth centuries, and in the eighth century the persecutions of the Paulicians on the charge of heresy, and the subsequent persecution of their spiritual descendants, the Albigenses and the Waldenses, who from Toulouse, and the valleys of the Alps, had spread largely over Southern Europe, there had been no movements of deviation from the line of belief prescribed by the church, though there had been many, and some remarkable instances, of personal effort to bring about reforms in the church.

During the thirteenth century, the good and fearless English bishop, Robert Greathead, reproved the worldly-minded canons of his cathedral of Lincoln; this led to an angry disputation, and the bishop of Lincoln determined to go to Avignon, and lay the matter before the pope. During his stay at Avignon, the spirit of Bishop Greathead was stirred within him at beholding the corrupt state of ecclesiastical society.

The English bishop was invited to preach before the Holy Father and his Court. The bishop preached, but not with enticing words of man's wisdom; in the simple majesty of truth, he enforced the necessity of obedience to Christian duty, insisting that the higher the position a man held in the church, the more pressing were the obligations of duty upon him. Bishop Greathead did not hesitate to declare that if the Holy Father allowed himself to be moved by any motives whatsoever, contrary to the teachings of Christ and his Apostles, he thereby separated himself from the body of Christ, which is the Church. The bishop went further and affirmed that obedience to a pope, who has by wrong doing severed himself from the body of Christ, is apostasy to Christ.

On his return to England, Bishop Greathead placed the secular affairs of his diocese in the hands of the civil authorities and gave himself entirely to the work of general pastor and Christian teacher. He visited every part of his diocese, preaching in country places, and in every city, town and hamlet.

The pope sent to the bishop of Lincoln a mandate, ordering him to confer upon an Italian youth, a favorite with the pope, a benefice in his diocese. To the mandate of the pope, the bishop replied: "No consideration can induce me to confer a benefice upon any one who is not qualified to perform its duties." This reply exasperated the pope; he vowed that the contumacious bishop of Lincoln should feel the weight of his power, but the cardinals held him back. They knew the independent spirit of the English church, and they feared the augmented force of public discontent which would be called forth if the pope were to issue a bull of excommunication against the bishop of Lincoln. They knew that Robert of Lincoln was greatly beloved and highly esteemed as a preacher and as a theologian.

Matthew, of Paris, writes: "After the death of Bishop Greathead, the pope determined to avenge himself by having the body of the bishop removed from consecrated ground, but before the order was issued, in a dream the pope saw the bishop of Lincoln standing before him, regarding him with a stern countenance, and, raising his crosier, struck him sharply on the side. For several days, the pope affirmed, he felt the smart of the blow from the bishop's crosier." No order of disinterment was issued, the remains of the undaunted bishop continued to rest peacefully in the God's-acre at Lincoln, while the influence of his spirit was a beacon light, beckoning men on to seek truth in Christian doctrine and holiness in Christian life.

Though a hundred years lay between, John Wycliffe was the son—in the gospel—of Robert Greathead. Wycliffe was rector of Lutterworth, in the diocese of Lincoln; he was a man of "vast understanding, invincible courage and indefatigable zeal." His preaching and writing were as subversive of existing prejudices and interests, as they were in keeping with genuine Christianity. Not only in England but on the Continent, the writings of Wycliffe were spiritual seeds that bore valuable fruit in the Master's vineyard. John Huss and Jerome, of Prague and other reformers and martyrs were his spiritual children. Their teachings and their death so moved on the hearts and the minds of the men of the German states that when, in riper times, the great German reformer appeared, a host of efficient friends stood staunchly by him.

When the righteous wrath of Dr. Martin Luther, aroused by Tetzel's nefarious traffic in indulgencies, led him to propound his immortal theses, he had no more thought of separating from the church than had Dr. Robert Greathead, bishop of Lincoln, when he preached his fearless sermon in the presence of the pope. And Luther was walking in the spiritual path pointed out by the bishop of Lincoln, when he renounced communion with the papal church. In the presence of pope and cardinals the bishop had declared that obedience to a pope who, by wrong doing, had severed himself from the body of Christ, was apostasy to Christ.

Previous to the conference with Cajetan, Luther's sole object was reformation in the church. He fondly believed that when the shameless abuse of the papal prerogative became known to the pope he would not only disavow all participation in the infamous traffic, but would issue a brief against the abuse.

That his fond belief was unfounded, that his hope of reformation in the church did not, under existing circumstances, come within the scope of things attainable, was made evident through the conference at Augsburg. The conduct of that conference plainly revealed the papal purpose to silence the opposers of a scheme which so readily filled the papal coffers, as well as those of an ambitious and unchristian archbishop.

When Pope Leo X. first learned of Luther's stand against the sale of indulgences he did not regard it as a matter worthy of serious consideration, thinking that an outburst of indignation from an overscrupulous monk would soon expend itself, and he might henceforth be kept silent by the force of elegant sarcasm, or the prospect of a bishop's mitre. But the pope had soon to learn that the cause of reform in Germany, though mainly voiced by one man, was staunchly supported by a formidable number of adherents, and against such a cause elegant sarcasm was a worthless weapon, and a bishop's mitre an unheeded bribe; notwithstanding the pope could not divest himself of the idea that to silence Brother Martin by inducing or compelling him to retract, or by excommunication, would be to nip in the bud the flower of reform.

In order to lead Luther to retract by favor or by force he sent Cardinal Cajetan to Augsburg, and cited Luther to appear before him in that city to discuss the points in dispute.

In obedience to the pope's mandate Luther repaired to Augsburg, and presented himself before Cardinal Cajetan. In the early conferences the manner of the cardinal was considerate and gentle. He desired by a show of affection to induce Brother Martin to retract, but not being able to stifle the conscientious scruples of the intrepid reformer with his cloak of kind seeming, he appealed to the authority of the church to compel the obstinate Saxon monk to retract. But neither persuasive affection nor the thunder of authority were sufficient to make Martin Luther recreant to the truth as it is in Christ. Luther desired to discuss the points at issue in Christian charity, but the cardinal did not wish discussion nor investigation. His purpose was to induce or compel Luther to give up the ground he had taken, to retract all he had preached and published against what he termed the corruptions of the church, and to return as a penitent to her bosom. To the cardinal's reiterated order, "Retract," the dauntless reformer answered, "Convince me of wrong, and I am ready to renounce the wrong. I stand by the word of God, by the whole word of God, and by none other than the word of God."

CHAPTER XIX.

DIET OF WORMS.

LUTHER perceived the uselessness and the danger of prolonging the conference, and by the aid of friends he quietly left Augsburg and returned to his post at Wittenberg.

Finding that Luther was beyond the grasp of his power, the Cardinal grew angry and vindictive; he and the friends of Tetzel joined forces to induce Pope Leo X. to issue a Brief against Dr. Martin Luther, condemning his teachings, adjudging his writings to the flames, and ordering him to confess his faults and to seek the clemency of the pope within sixty days or he would be cast out of the church. This Brief determined Dr. Martin Luther to withdraw from the papal church before Pope Leo X. could issue the bull of excommunication against him. And in order that his withdrawal from the church of Rome should be generally known, he posted up a public announcement that on the next morning at nine o'clock the papal law books and the papal Brief would be burned in front of the Elster gate. A multitude were present to witness the scene; with Luther came Melanchthon and a number of other doctors and masters. On the burning pile Luther flung first the decretals and then the papal Brief. By that act Dr. Martin Luther declared himself no longer subject to the Pope of Rome; for whoever, according to the custom of the times, publicly burned the statute book of his sovereign thereby declared that he was no longer subject to his authority.

After Luther had taken this decisive step, he began with renewed ardor to confirm the doctrines he had taught.

And his powerful teaching was as new life-breath to the souls of the people, who began to see more clearly the depth and the simplicity of the doctrines he taught, to feel the need of going directly to the Father in heaven, through Jesus the Saviour of men, for pardon of sin and for grace to help in every time of need.

Dr. Martin Luther's beloved and constant friend was Dr. Philip Melanchthon. Melanchthon stood by Luther with the cherishing love of a brother through all the labors and the perils of the Reformation. Melanchthon's discreetness and gentleness tempered the zeal and intrepid courage of Luther, and in turn the ardent, undaunted spirit of Luther gave firmness and vigor to the gentler spirit of Melanchthon. Luther was wont to say, "The Apology of Philip Melanchthon is worth all the writings of all the doctors of the church put together, not excepting those of St. Augustine, though amongst them St. Augustine unquestionably holds the first place."

After the election of Charles V. as Emperor the first Congress or Diet was held in the city of Worms. The pope had sent a Brief to the Emperor demanding that he should enforce the bull of excommunication issued against Martin Luther under an imperial edict. The Emperor so far acceded to the urgent demand of the pope that he caused to be drawn up and laid before the Diet a proposition to the effect that Martin Luther should be arrested and his protectors tried for high treason. The Diet would not consider the proposition, but by a general vote of that body it was conceded that Dr. Martin Luther should be cited to appear before the Diet to give information concerning his doctrines and his books, and further, should the said Dr. Martin Luther fail to obey the citation he should henceforth be treated as an avowed heretic.

On receiving the summons Luther expressed his readiness to obey, and with three friends set out for

Worms. On the forenoon of April 16, 1521, Luther entered the city of Worms. He and his three friends were in an open carriage, accompanied by a large number of men on horseback; thousands of people thronged the streets to get a look at the famous man.

On the day after his arrival he was to appear before the Diet. At the appointed time the street from the house of the Knights of St. John, where Luther lodged, to the palace where the Diet was in session was so thronged with spectators eager to get a look at the reformer, that he and his friends had to make their way through a side street. As he entered the hall of the palace the distinguished warrior, Von Frundsberg, clapped him on the shoulder, saying: "My poor monk, my poor monk, thou art on thy way to make such a stand as I and my knights have never done in my toughest battles. But if thou art sure of the justice of thy cause, go forward in the name of God, and be of good courage."

The abruptness of the questions put by the imperial official, Eck, caused Luther to ask for time for deliberation; he was granted until the afternoon of the next day.

When on the following day his case was called the questions were asked, "Will you defend *all* that is written in your books, or will you recant some portions of them?" "I have divided my books," answered Luther, "into three classes. In the first class I have set forth simple, evangelical truths, professed alike by friend and foe; on no account could I retract any part of these. In the second class I have attacked corrupt laws and doctrines of the papacy, which no one can deny have tormented and martyred the conscience of Christians; to retract these would be to make myself a cloak for weakness and tyranny. In the third class I have written against individuals who endeavored to subvert godly doctrine and to shield tyranny; in these I may at times have been more violent than was befitting, but to retract them would be to abet godlessness and tyranny. In defence of my books I can only say in the words of the Lord Jesus Christ, 'If I have spoken evil, bear witness of the evil, but if well, why smitest thou me?'"

Luther's speech was conclusive and respectful; he closed with an earnest warning to the emperor, and to the electors, of the danger of trying to promote peace, by condemnation of the Divine Word.

The courage, the clearness, and the modest candor of the speech, delighted every fair-minded man of the Diet, but to the prejudiced, it was cause of offence; the official Eck, commissioned by the emperor, reproved him for having spoken impertinently, but at the same time held out the promise, that if he would retract the offensive articles, his other writings should be dealt with fairly. Eck demanded of Luther a plain answer, without horns, whether or not he would retract. "I will give you an answer," replied Luther, "with neither horns nor teeth; unless I am refuted from the Scriptures, or by evident reason, I cannot retract; my conscience is bound to adhere to truth, to the Word of God. It is clear that popes and councils have erred and contradicted themselves, and therefore, upon such authority, I cannot and will not retract anything; my conscience must be clear before God."

After some further discussion, Luther concluded with the words that grew into the hearts of his followers, "Here I stand; I can do no otherwise; God help me. Amen."

That evening the emperor closed the Diet; he granted to Luther a safe conduct for twenty-one days, with the command that he should not preach on his way back to Wittenberg.

The Elector of Saxony, Frederic the Wise, saw clearly that Luther had nothing to hope from the favor of the emperor; the elector was attached to Luther and to his cause, but did not wish to draw upon himself and upon Saxony the displeasure of the emperor in this strait, so he devised means to get Dr. Martin safely out of the way for a time, until conditions were less threatening.

Dr. Luther was informed of the plan of the elector; it was not a plan to his liking, but his affection and deference toward the elector overmastered his dislike of the arrangement. April 26th he left Worms, and on his journey he stopped at several places to visit friends and relations, and without regard to the command of the emperor, he preached three times at different places, not daring, he affirmed, to permit the Word of God to be bound.

In the gathering twilight of Saturday, May 4th, as his carriage entered the wooded heights, beyond Altenstein, armed horsemen dashed out of the wood, and with terrible threats, ordered the driver to stop on the instant; the horsemen pulled Luther out of the carriage, pushed him on a horse and hurried him off at full speed, leaving the terrified driver to go on his way unmolested.

About eleven, in the thick darkness of the night, the horsemen with their prisoner reached the Fortress of Wartburg.

Soon the news flew over the country that Dr. Luther had been seized and carried off by his enemies, news which filled the hearts of thousands with profound grief; meanwhile Luther was held at the Wartburg as Knight prisoner. On reaching the Fortress he had to lay aside his monkish garb and assume the dress of a Knight and let a full beard grow. In the castle he was known as the Knight George. Cranach's wood-cut of the Knight George shows an ample mustache and a full curling beard. As Knight prisoner he was treated with highest consideration, the apartments of the castle were free to him, and in the company of a trusty servant he was permitted to take walks and rides in the surrounding country.

After Luther had left Worms, the papal legate, by commission of the emperor, prepared an edict against Luther, to go into effect at the expiration of the safe conduct granted by the emperor. In addition to the setting forth of the bull of excommunication, the Edict declared that wherever the heretic Dr. Martin Luther was found, he was to be taken captive and handed over to the emperor.

The Edict of Worms shows to advantage the wisdom of the wise Frederic.

Luther, safe in the Wartburg, as Knight George, had the privilege of communicating by letter with his friends in Wittenberg, through Spalatin, the spiritual advisor of the elector.

For the comfort and edification of his friends in Wittenberg, Luther wrote an exposition of the thirty-seventh psalm, which was sent under cover to Spalatin. In the quiet of his seclusion he was continuously at work writing expositions of scripture and other works, in order to impress on the hearts and minds of his people a fuller conception of Christian duty and Christian privileges. To his father he dedicated a work on monastic vows in consideration of his father's protest against his entering a convent.

But Luther longed for active work; he complained that he had to sit idly in his Patmos, declaring that he would rather go to the stake in the active service of God than to stagnate in that solitude.

But meanwhile, in the outer world, the religious movement he had started took such deep hold on the people that it continued to grow and strengthen, not only in Wittenberg but through the country generally, notwithstanding the Edict of Worms had been published in the states, cities and towns of the empire.

In addition to the feeling of solitude which oppressed Luther, his mind was ill at ease on account of the news that reached him from without of the wild fanaticism that had broken out at Zwickau, and of the passionate forces which had been aroused by Carlstadt in Wittenberg. Luther believed that Carlstadt's course brought discredit on the gospel. This so stirred his oppressed spirit that, contrary to the advice of the elector, he resolved to leave the Wartberg.

His final departure from the fortress was on March 1st. He journeyed through Jena to Borna, where he lodged with a city official. From Borna, he wrote to the elector, informing him of his resolve to throw himself entirely on God, and in that trust to return to Wittenberg. Luther writes: "I shall return under a far higher protection than yours; nay, I hold that I can offer your highness a surer protection than your highness can offer me. God only is the worker here, therefore he who has the most faith will be able to give the most protection."

Luther reached Wittenberg safely on March 6th, and on the Sunday following, to the great joy of his congregation, he preached in his old pulpit; and with his accustomed zeal he threw himself into his work in all its branches, both in the church and in the university.

Together with Melanchthon and a few other co-workers, he revised his translation into German of the New Testament. The work was completed by September, and in reference to that Testament, an opponent, Cocklæus, writing shortly after its appearance says, "Luther's New Testament is multiplied by the printers in a most remarkable manner; shoemakers, women and any and every lay person who can read German, read that Testament greedily as the fountain of all truth, and by repeated readings they so impress it on their memories that they quote scripture even to the doctors of theology."

Luther, with Melanchthon, Bugenhagen and a few others, then began to translate into German the Hebrew Bible. To translate the Old Bible was a far more difficult work, and required the labor of several years to complete it. To give to a people the Bible in their native tongue is to bestow upon them an inestimable blessing.

CHAPTER XX.
CHARACTERISTICS OF LUTHER.

THE new literature of Germany opens with Luther, Reuchlin and Erasmus. The corrected Greek texts of the New Testament by Reuchlin, and the more widely known corrected and revised texts of Erasmus, gave to scholars a purified version of the New Testament, but Luther gave the whole Bible to the *people* by translating it into their native tongue. Early in the year 1524 Luther published the German hymn-book. It was a small book, containing only eight hymns; of these, three were adaptations from the psalms, the others were his compositions. During the year, he added twenty more of his hymns, and still later twelve more, among them that grand hymn beginning, "A mighty Fortress is our God."

Soon other poetic natures were inspired to follow his example, and a full German hymn-book went forth to all the churches in cities in towns and in country places, and it went also into the homes of the people. In his preface Luther says, "I am not of opinion that the gospel should be employed to strike down and destroy all the arts. I would rather that all the arts, especially music, should be employed in the service of Him who created them and gave them to man."

Luther earnestly counseled the importance of affording a liberal education to the young. He recommends that the cloisters of the mendicant orders should be converted into schools for boys and girls.

In contemplating the character of Dr. Martin Luther we perceive that he was a remarkable coalescence of the opposite elements in human nature. "The gravel and the gold rolled together in the rich channel of his mind, and he made no effort to exhibit the one or to conceal the other." Luther was a practical man of action, and he was a dreamy mystic; he was brusque, even to roughness, and he was capable of exquisite tenderness; he was the very soul of obstinacy, yet always open to conviction. Heine says, "Luther was unconquerable as the storm that uproots the oak, and he was gentle as the zephyr that dallies with the violet."

Krauth says, "Luther won the trophies of power and the garlands of affection; potentates feared him, and little children played with him. He has monuments in marble and bronze, medals in silver and in gold, but his noblest monument is the best love of the best hearts, and the purest impression of his image has been left on the souls of regenerated nations. He knew how to command, for he had learned to obey. Had he been less courageous, he would have attempted nothing; had he been less cautious, he would have ruined all; the torrent was resistless, but the banks were deep." The eloquent Catholic Bishop, Bossuet, writing of Luther, says, "He possessed a strength of genius, a vehemence in discourse, a living and impetuous eloquence, which entranced and ravished the people." And again Bishop Bossuet writes, "Luther was the trumpet, or rather the thunder, the lightning, which has roused the world from its lethargy. It was not so much Luther who spoke, as God, whose lightning burst from his lips."

Luther rejected the aid of the sword; during his life there was no war. His watchwords were, truth and right must conquer.

The two men whose lives and labors have exerted the most important and far-reaching influence on the Western world, an influence destined to be felt to earth's remotest bounds, were a Jew of Tarsus and a German monk.

The gospel of Christ, so faithfully taught by the

great Jew, in season and out of season, had, in the onward march of the ages, been perverted from its course of pure blessing and turned into the channel of superstition. Human perversity, narrowness, ignorance and ambition had changed the spirit of brotherly helpfulness into that of cruel oppression. Everywhere men groaned under the yoke of superstition and of despotism.

The German monk, with intrepid hand, broke the chain which bound men under the heavy yoke of religious superstition, and with his clarion voice aroused them to resist the intolerance of mere authority and to base both their belief and action on the eternal principles of right,—of Christian truth.

The principles which Luther labored to reinstate have had a three-fold development; through the enfranchisement of the human mind, Christianity has been interpreted to human reason; the thoughtful study of scripture, on which he so strenuously insisted, has given rise to biblical criticism, and resistance to the intolerance of mere authority has led to constitutional liberty.

In the German reformation, the towering figure of Martin Luther fills the fore-front; in the Swiss reformation, no one figure stands so conspicuously forth; there are several leaders, but foremost among them stands Ulrich Zwinglius, who has been aptly termed the Apostle of Switzerland.

The reformation in Germany began with the earnest efforts of one man against a glaring abuse; in Switzerland, there was united action among several men whose souls had been illuminated with the light of the gospel, but they looked to Zwinglius as the prime mover in the great work.

In the German reformation the tendency was from one point to extend out and include many; in the Swiss reformation the line of action was from diversity to unity.

CHAPTER XXI.

ULRICH ZWINGLI.

LOOKING back to the early years of the ministry of Ulrich Zwinglius, or Zwingli, we may trace the steps by which he was gradually led on to the great work of reformation in his native republic.

When, in the year 1515, Francis I. invaded Italy, the pope sent to the Swiss cantons, or states, to enlist in his cause the brave Swiss, who, on previous occasions, had served him so valiantly. To the call of the pope the Swiss soldiery promptly responded. Ulrich Zwingli was then parish priest at Glaris, and among the Swiss an ancient custom made it the duty of priests to attend the army in order to celebrate divine service, to assist the dying, and by their presence and exhortations to lessen the disorder to which soldiers are generally inclined. When called by the soldiers of Glaris to go with them, not for a moment did Zwingli shirk the duty, though he disapproved of war except in defense of home and country, and it was a sad break in his cherished habits of study.

The opportunity afforded by his marches in Italy to become acquainted with Italian society opened his eyes to a condition of which he had not dreamed, and the church he found to be no better than the world; the lower clergy were ignorant and avaricous, the higher clergy were ambitious, faithless and most corrupt. Zwingli was pierced with sharp convictions of the pressing necessity of reform in the church. On his return home, he prayerfully sought to learn the will of the Lord as to the needful steps to be taken for the redemption of the church. For his part, he began to apply himself with renewed diligence to the study of the scriptures and of the early fathers, and the nearer he traced Christianity to its fountainhead, the life and teachings of Christ, the simpler he found its doctrines and mode of worship. To succeeding ages he traced the accumulated multitude of observances, with which he found it encumbered. Through the scriptures light began to dawn on his soul, but he was so penetrated with the importance of the subject that he could not dare to take for granted any conclusion for which he could not find clear proof in scripture. He also took up the writings of Arnold, of Brescia, Wycliffe and other reformers. The writings of Wycliffe particularly attracted him and helped to mould his religious views, as they had done those of John Huss and Jerome of Prague. But the political factions encroached upon his time and interrupted his studies, and though his parishioners were warmly attached to him, they rendered his position among them undesirable by their constant political agitations.

In the quiet abbey of Einsiedlen the monk, who had been Baron von Geroldseck, had risen to the first post in the abbey, and was known as the administrator. He was a man of ability and of superior learning, and he delighted to draw around him men of learning, zealous for the truth, to assist him in his efforts to elevate the character of the priesthood. Zwingli's reputation as an able preacher and a man of spotless integrity attracted him, and he offered the young pastor the position of chief preacher in the abbey. The offer came to Zwingli as a heaven-sent boon; the position would not only afford him ample leisure for study, but at Einsiedlen he would come into association with the leading scholars of the Cantons.

Zwingli remained at Einsiedlen three years; they were to him valuable years, knowledge and strength-gaining years; positive convictions succeeded the doubts and fears which had disturbed him at Glaris. The administrator was his attached and admiring friend, and, acting under Zwingli's advice, he made many reforms demanded by the lessening credulity of the people consequent upon the re-birth of learning. Zwingli had also, at Einsiedlen, a few choice friends; together they studied the scriptures, the fathers, the schoolmen, and the works of Reuchlin and of Erasmus; they discussed the new and bold ideas, found in these works, and subjected them to searching examinations. Together they lamented the corrupt and superstitious practices so prevalent in the church and prevailing to such an extent even there in the abbey, on the quiet mountain height of Einsiedlen.

The influence of the Renaissance, which had so largely aroused to renewed activity the minds of persons who lived in or near the centres of culture, had scarcely been felt by the rural population of remote and mountainous districts. There at Einsiedlen, multitudes of men and women toiled up the rugged mountain paths, to prostrate themselves in the chapel of the wonder-working image of Mary, and out of their offerings the salary of the preacher was paid. The enlightenment of this multitude of worshipers might leave the preacher to starve. But such a possibility did not damp the ardor of Zwingli's religious zeal. To the multitude assembled in the chapel, he declared in words of eloquent warning, that vain was their trust in the image they adored; it could work no miracles, it could pardon no sins, it was powerless to grant salvation. "Your toilsome pilgrimages, your offerings, are all in vain," cried the preacher; "God is with you at your homes as really, as truly, as He is with you here in the chapel of Our Lady of Einsiedlen; pardon and salvation are only to be attained through living faith in our Lord Jesus Christ." The number of pilgrimages so decidedly decreased, that the pilgrim worshipers no longer came in multitudes.

In his course of preaching, Zwingli continued with fearless and convincing eloquence to assail and expose the superstitious practices sanctioned by the church. Still he remained on friendly terms with the clerical dignitaries about him. These friendly relations may in part be attributable to the magnetic charm of his lovable nature and gentle manners, but they are chiefly due to the sagacity of the papal legates, who estimated correctly Zwingli's far-reaching influence with the people, and they determined by kind toleration toward him, and some outward reforms, to hold him constant to the church, and through his influence to bind the Swiss Cantons steadily to their papal alliance. The papal legate, Pucci, was particularly kind and courteous to Zwingli; he made no complaint of his sermons against penance, costly offerings, prayers to the virgin and to the saints, nor of his repeated assurances to his congregations that "when the heart is estranged from God, all these things avail them nothing." The legate assured him that the holy father felt deeply the necessity of reform, and promised on his return to Rome to present to his Holiness the correct condition of affairs in the church, and he felt confident that the holy father would not fail to institute such measures, as in the end would effect the much-needed reforms.

The cardinal legate returned to Rome, but nothing grew out of his promises. Zwingli saw that it was a vain hope to look to the princes of the church for the inauguration of movements tending to thorough reform. He was more and more convinced that only the faithful preaching of the Word of God could awaken the dormant spiritual life of the church.

Among the friends whom Zwingli made at Einsiedlen was Myconius, professor of Greek in the school of Zurich. Zurich was one of the largest and most important of the cities of Switzerland, and Myconius thought that the power and eloquence of Zwingli ought to be exerted in a larger field than that of Einsiedlen. On several occasions Myconius had induced Zwingli to visit Zurich, and on these occasions, his preaching had produced a deep impression.

When the important post of cathedral preacher became vacant, Myconius proposed Zwingli, and he was duly elected, though not without opposition, and a notification of his election was sent him. Shortly thereafter, in December, 1518, Zwingli left Einsiedlen, deeply regretted by the Administrator, by his intimate friends, and by his parishioners generally. On his arrival in Zurich, he was received by the cathedral chapter with every mark of respect, though some of the Canons had opposed his election. At the first meeting of the chapter Zwingli declared to them his purpose to entirely consecrate himself and his ministry to the service of God, that his main object should be "to instruct in the true faith the souls committed to my care; to the glory of our God and Saviour." Such consecration was not in consonance with the views of the opposing canons; they regarded the first duty of the cathedral preacher to be diligence in collecting the revenues of the cathedral.

Zwingli began his ministerial labors by a course of sermons on the gospel according to St. Matthew. "Too long," said Zwingli, "have the life and teachings of our blessed Saviour been a dead letter to the people." The cathedral was crowded with eager listeners from all the grades of society, scholars, statesmen, and humblest burghers. He expounded the gospel in his sermons, chapter by chapter, mostly in language plain and familiar, so that none could fail to understand, but at times rising to sublime heights of eloquence. From belief and faith in the Lord Jesus Christ, he passed to the practices of life; and as at Glaris and Einsiedlen, he entered an earnest and fearless protest against mercenary military service, and against the acceptance of pensions from foreign princes; "these pensions," said the preacher, "are the bane of our country; they bring into our Swiss Cantons, extravagance, intemperance, and lawlessness."

One of the opposing canons tried to show him how unwise was such a mode of preaching.

"It will do more harm than good to follow up this new method," affirmed Canon Hoffman. "It is not a new method," answered Zwingli. "It is the old method, the method of the early fathers, and of St. Chrysostom, and it is the method of St. Augustine."

The Swiss reformation was now fairly started, and it moved steadily on, though under the pressure of many difficulties, the lamentations of some of Zwingli's colleagues, the reproaches of quondam friends, and the fury of the monks. Against the Franciscan monk, Sampson, the vender of indulgences, Zwingli declared from the cathedral pulpit, "no man, priest nor pope, has the power to forgive sin, only God can do that."

CHAPTER XXII.

THE SWISS REFORMATION.

IN the year 1520, Pope Leo X. had declared forty-one of the propositions of Luther to be heretical, and in 1521 the diet of Worms declared that he should be treated as a heretic, and threatened severe penalties against those who might afford him aid or succor. Late in the year 1522, the bishop of Constance appealed to the general Swiss diet to assist him in preserving obedience in his diocese. The canton and city of Zurich were in his diocese, and Zwingli knew that this was specially leveled against him; so early in the year 1523 he appeared before the great council of Zurich and petitioned the council to order a public conference of the clergy of Zurich and of the deputies of the bishop of Constance in order that he and his brother reformers might render an account of their doctrine. He promised on his own part and that of his brother reformers to retract whatever they had preached or written, which could be proven contrary to scripture. The council approved the proposition and addressed a circular letter to the clergy of the city and canton of Zurich, ordering them to appear at the town hall on the day next after the festival of Charlemagne; and they sent a letter to the bishop of Constance announcing the conference and begging that his deputies might be present on the occasion.

Meanwhile Zwingli prepared and published seventy-six articles as the basis of discussion. His first article, without alluding to it, combated the generally received assertion of St. Augustine, "If the church had not approved the gospel, I should not believe it." Zwingli's first article declared, "It is an error to assert that the gospel is nothing without the approbation of the church; no other teachings, no matter from what source they come, are of equal force with the teachings of the gospel." The articles following were equally brief and forceful; the last article declared, "The church has no right to molest any person on account of his opinions; it is the duty of the state to arrest all disturbers of the public peace." At the appointed time the conference assembled, the deputies of the bishop of Constance being present. Zwingli's articles were presented and accepted as the subjects of discussion. In answer to the arguments of Zwingli, the deputies of the bishop of Constance desired to base their arguments on canon law,—the decrees of church councils; but Zwingli refused to admit as proof evidence drawn from canon law; he could accept no proof that was not contained in sacred scripture.

The conference closed leaving the disputants in the same position toward each other as when it began, but the simple and clear setting forth of the reformed doctrine produced a decided effect upon the people, and upon the members of the great council.

After the adjournment of the conference the council held a deliberation and then formulated their final decision, the decree of the great council of the canton and city of Zurich, "Whereas, Ulrich Zwingli and his brethren have not been confuted nor convicted of heresy, they shall continue to preach the gospel as they have heretofore done; and be it further enacted that the pastors of the canton and city of Zurich shall draw their doctrines only from the sacred scriptures, and that they abstain from bitter controversies and personal reflections." The Swiss reformation was no longer the innovations of a few pastors, it was in Zurich a national movement authorized by the highest secular authority.

But being convinced that no human force can command conviction, Zwingli would not use the power with which he was invested to compel changes in the mode of worship. Many of the churches retained their pictures and images and continued to celebrate mass. But among the reformed were many who lacked the wise moderation of Zwingli; impetuous and vehement, they declaimed against what they called idolatry, and wrought up some of the weaker sort to such a pitch of excitement that they wanted to pull down every picture and dash down every image. But Zwingli's moderation prevailed, and he calmed the excitement of the people, though it still burned in the bosoms of a few men, who pulled down a crucifix at the gate of the city. At this act the opponents raised a hue and cry against the perpetrators, they were arrested, and there arose a clamor for their death as guilty of sacrilege; Zwingli defended them against the charge of sacrilege, but considered them as deserving of punishment for taking authority in their own hands and acting without the sanction of the government. The chief instigator was banished for two years and the others were imprisoned for three months. In the autumn of the same year, 1523, the great council ordered another conference, that by means of the discussion the council might be able to decide whether the worship of images was authorized by the scriptures, and whether according to the scriptures the mass should be observed or abolished. Invitations to be present at the conference were sent by the council to the bishops of Constance, Coire and Basle, and all the Swiss cantons were requested by the great council of Zurich to send deputies to the important conference to be held in the city of Zurich. The bishops declined the invitations, but the bishop of Constance sent to the conference a written defence of the mass and of the use of images. "The mass," contended the bishop, "is a necessary consecration and oblation, without which the Eucharist is not truly celebrated. Images are not idols of false gods, they are the likenesses of saints whose lives were a blessing to the world, and who have been received into heaven, and the homage paid to them serves to nourish piety." As the bishop of Constance had cited no scriptural proofs, nor advanced any new arguments from the early fathers, the council decided that his paper afforded no ground for discussion. Of the cantons but few responded to the invitations sent.

The conference, numbering over nine hundred men, prelates, theologians, clergy and laity, assembled on the appointed day, October 28th; two deputies from St. Gaul and one from Schaffhausen were chosen to preside over the deliberations of the conference. The paper from the bishop of Constance was submitted, but as it contained no proofs from scripture it was laid on the table. Zwingli and his fellow-student at Einsiedlen, Leo Jude, were appointed to answer those who defended the mass as a sacrifice, and the worship of images. The prior of the Augustines, a famous preacher, and warmly attached to what he termed ancient orthodoxy, first took up the line of defence, and eloquently and logically argued from canon law; but Zwingli and Jude refused to accept any proof not drawn from scripture. The subjects under discussion were argued for and against for three days; during the discussion the Augustine prior confessed that he could not refute the theses of Zwingli unless he were always allowed to have resource to canon law.

In conclusion Zwingli insisted that "the magnificence of churches and the rich vestments of the higher clergy strike the senses and heighten the pomp of worship, but do not lead the mind to serious meditation nor to communion of soul with Him whose invisible glory should fill the temples dedicated to his worship."

The discussion made a deep impression on the minds of the hearers; there could be no question of the victory of the two reformers, Zwingli and Jude.

The council dismissed the conference with thanks

for the readiness with which their summons had been obeyed, but they reserved their final decision until they had calmly deliberated upon the matter under consideration.

Zwingli continued to labor by writing and by preaching to procure the abolition of the mass and the banishment of images from the churches. He wrote and preached that "the doctrine of the invocation of the saints is a dangerous instrument in the hands of unlearned and unscrupulous priests, and that the false ideas of the people could only be overcome by the removal of the objects of their superstition." After duly considering the matter the great council determined to undertake the reformation of worship, and in the beginning of the following year, 1524, they began by granting to individuals the right to remove from the churches any pictures or statues which had been presented by their ancestors or by themselves. At the expiration of the time granted for such removals the council appointed two magistrates, whose duty it should be to visit all the churches and have every remaining picture and statue removed. Among those who grieved at what they regarded as the desecration of the churches were a few who were measurably happy in the belief that the sacred images would of themselves return to the churches and resume their places. But "hope deferred maketh the heart sick," and after expectant and continually disappointed waiting, these people gave up their belief in the images. The example of the capital was not only followed in the canton of Zurich, but several other cantons enlisted under the banner of reform; but in yet other cantons, especially the five forest cantons, much indignation was manifested, stirred up by the monks; the people of Zurich were denounced as insulters of the saints. But undaunted, the city and canton of Zurich held on their way. The great council proceeded to suppress the mendicant orders on account of the indolent lives and pernicious example of the monks. The council declared that young and robust monks should learn trades and become useful citizens of the state, that those who were given to studious life should be furnished with the means to prosecute their studies, and those who were aged and those who were infirm should for their support be granted annuities and a home should be provided for them in the Franciscan convent. The convent of the Dominicans, by order of the council, was made a hospital and its large revenues devoted to the maintenance of the sick poor of both the city and canton of Zurich. The convent of the Augustines was turned into a public school.

These arrangements were wise and disinterested; they do credit to the Council of Zurich and to Ulrich Zwingli, their chief adviser. The mass was abolished, and, soon after, the sacrament of the Lord's Supper was celebrated in accordance with the simple mode of apostolic days; the bread and the wine were administered to all communicants. Zwingli taught that the bread and the wine in the sacred supper were symbolical, even as water is in baptism. He rejected both the doctrine of transubstantiation and of consubstantiation, or real presence. "The supper of our Lord," said Zwingli, "is a sacrament of commemoration, and signifies the spiritual communion between Christ and the communicant; and is the most hallowed of the Christian sacraments."

Previous to the anabaptist outburst of fanatical enthusiasm Luther had declared, "It is not the sacrament of our Lord's supper which sanctifies, it is faith in the sacrament." But the extravagancies of those unreasoning enthusiasts produced a modification in his views; he rejected papal transubstantiation, but he insisted on the real presence of Christ in the bread and the wine; some writers term this doctrine consubstantiation. This difference of belief between Luther and Zwingli, who personally were entire strangers the one to the other, inaugurated a long war of pamphlets between their followers which generated much bitterness of spirit. This deplorable division among Protestants induced that ardent protestant Philip, Landgrave of Hesse, to endeavor to bring about a union of all Protestants. To effect this great end he, in the autumn of 1529, invited Luther and Zwingli and the distinguished theologians of both sides to meet in conference at his castle of Marburg. Philip desired not only to heal the doctrinal divisions which kept the Protestant communities at variance, but also to form an armed coalition of all Protestant States against the papal forces. But, alas for his well-meant efforts! he could accomplish neither.

For the entertainment of the distinguished guests from whose conference he anticipated such important results he made royal preparations.

In the Marburg conference Luther showed the obstinate side of his great character; on the second day of the conference, the day when the disputants first met for general discussion, Luther said, "I protest that I differ from the Swiss in regard to the doctrine of our Lord's Supper, and that I shall always differ from them." Later in the discussion he avowed that he rejected reason, common sense and mathematical proof. The landgrave soon perceived that the union among Protestants he so ardently desired was a lost cause. The Saxon doctors refused to acknowledge the Swiss doctors as brethren; they would only acknowledge them as friends. To which the Swiss doctors replied, "We are conscious of having acted as in the presence of God. Posterity will be our witness. Let us on each side defend our belief without railing, and let us carefully avoid all harsh and violent words in writing and speaking."

When the parting hour came Luther approached Zwingli and the other Swiss doctors, saying, "I offer you the hand of peace and charity." The hand of peace and charity was eagerly grasped by the Swiss divines, though they would not abate one jot of what they held as sacred truth.

CHAPTER XXIII.

Union of Reformed Cantons.

The union of the reformed cantons, Zurich, Berne, Basle, St. Gaul, Schaffhausen and Appenzel, isolated them from the papal cantons, particularly from the five forest cantons. These cantons formed an alliance with King Ferdinand, and they banded themselves in a treaty to spare no efforts to suppress the reforms, or as they expressed it, the innovations of the heretical cantons within their borders.

In the terrible civil war which followed Zwingli went with the forces of Zurich as their chaplain; the people were unwilling to let him go. "Stay with us," urged the burgomaster, "we have need of you, the council needs you." "Not so," answered Zwingli, "I cannot remain quietly at home by my fireside while my brethren expose their lives. I must go with the army."

On the field of battle, while stooping to speak a few last words of prayer in the ear of a dying man, a stone hurled at him struck him on the head; other stones thrown in quick succession laid him prostrate; an ignoble foeman seeing him fall, thrust him through with his lance just as Zwingli was speaking his last words, "They can kill the body, they cannot kill the soul." With these words still hovering about his lips his soul passed from earth to heaven to meet his Lord and Saviour, whom he had so faithfully served upon earth.

The news of his death filled all Zurich with grief, and all the reformed cantons bewailed with Zurich the death of the great reformer. The untimely death of Ulrich Zwingli in the active prime of his life was an irreparable loss to the Swiss reformation.

As leader in the Swiss reformation, Zwingli was succeeded by John Calvin. The two men were of most unlike natures. Zwingli was warm-hearted, generous and forgiving; Calvin was cold, stern and relentless. Zwingli was not irritated by contradiction; Calvin was intolerant of contradiction. Zwingli held that conformity to the clear and precise teachings of the gospel should be required of Christians, on all other points individuals ought to think for themselves; Calvin held to the absolute sovereignty of logically deduced dogma. Zwingli's preaching was eloquent, persuasive, forceful, often vehement; Calvin's preaching was philosophical and exegetical.

Zwingli's last work was an abstract of his doctrine, addressed to the king of France, Francis I. The work was written but a few weeks before his lamented and untimely death. In that work the reader cannot fail to perceive a loving breadth of spirit and a mind rising above the narrowing influence of prejudice. The spirit which breathes through Zwingli's works leads Faith to look upward, and, with ear attent, to hear Zwingli singing with Faber:

"There's a wideness in God's mercy,
Like the wideness of the sea;
There's a kindness in His justice
Which is more than liberty."

Calvin was but eight years old when Luther posted up in Wittenberg his immortal theses, the first decisive step in the great German reformation. Calvin's father was a native of northern France, a grave, stern man; he was apostolic notary, and secretary to his bishop. It has been said, "The gravity of his father and the piety of his mother formed the basis of his stern and religious nature." As a young man, Calvin was won to the reformed doctrines while a student at Bourges. The professor of Greek at Bourges had seen and heard Luther, and he had studied the Greek Testament of Erasmus. The expositions given by that Greek professor, Melchior Wolmar, of the scriptures were to the young student an astounding revelation, and became the absorbing interest of his life. Speaking of himself at that time, he says, "I was so obstinately addicted to papal superstitions, it was hard to draw myself out of that slough." In 1529, we find him in Paris, a preacher of the reformed doctrine and pastor of a small church. One of the early seals to his ministry was the rector of the University of Paris, Nicholas Cop. On the following Martinmas, according to custom, the rector was to deliver the annual address. He asked Calvin to write it for him, and according to Beza, Calvin framed for him an address very different from what was customary, so different that it stirred up a commotion in the Sorbonne, and the parliament of France took up the matter and ordered the arrest of the rector, who, having timely warning, escaped and fled to Basle, in Switzerland. By some means the authorities learned that the offending address had been prepared by Calvin, and his arrest was ordered. He, too, escaped, and after a brief sojourn at places of safety in France and in Italy he went to Switzerland and settled at Basle. In this city his far-reaching work as a reformer was begun.

Luther and Zwingli took the Bible as their guide-book of faith and of conduct, their guide-book to heaven, and as its light shone upon them, warming their hearts and illuminating their minds, they preached and they wrote of the life-giving truths they had learned. But this was not Calvin's method, he preached the great doctrines of the reformation, but he was not ready to write until he could find in the scriptures a system of doctrine which to his mind would be logically satisfactory, and with that great logical hammer he desired at one giant blow to overthrow and destroy the whole superstructure of Rome. To this end, he wrote his "Institutes of the Christian Religion." The work was first published at Basle, 1536. But for twenty years thereafter he continued to labor on this, his greatest work, at Basle, at Strasburg and at Geneva. Not until 1559 was the last and completed edition of the great work published. It consists of four books. The first book treats of God in His work of creation; the second book, of Jesus Christ and His work of redemption; the third, of the Holy Spirit and His work of regeneration; the fourth, of the Church as the depository of the means of grace and salvation.

In treating of redemption, Calvin brings in his doctrine of predestination, which falls like a pall upon his theology. Calvin says, "God, in the fullness of His sovereignty, by His eternal and immutable counsel, has decreed one portion of the human family to salvation, and the other to damnation." "The elect have to bless and praise Him forever, and the reprobate have no right to complain; God was under no obligation to the elect nor to the reprobate." The election of grace had early been taught in the church, but Calvin states, that "to admit the election of grace and reject the election of reprobation is stupid folly." Calvin took for the basis of his terrible doctrine, a hard lifeless logic, a necessity of his system of establishing the absolute sovereignty of God.

No system of logical induction, however closely knit, can elucidate the plan and purposes of infinite wisdom. The logic, by which Calvin has attempted to trace and define the "infinite plan," is as hard and dead as an Egyptian mummy. But the responsibility of the dread doctrine of predestination should not be thrown wholly on Calvin. St. Augustine, in a milder manner, but just as surely, states the same doctrine.

From Basle, Calvin was called in 1536 to Geneva, as pastor of a church and professor of divinity; this was shortly after the first issue of his Institutes. His ministrations in Geneva were faithful and courageous, but severely strict, his inflexible strictness irritated the majority of the people against him, and in two years time they succeeded in having sentence of banishment pronounced against him and his friend and fellow pastor, Farel. Calvin again sought refuge at Basle and Farel went with him. From Basle, Calvin was called to Strasburg as preacher and professor of theology. His lectures soon attracted a great number of students, and he was held in such high esteem, that he was presented with the freedom of the city; still toward Geneva he turned his longing eyes, and wrote many letters to his friends there.

From Strasburg he sent his famous answer to the cooing-dove notes of Sadolet, secretary of Pope Leo X., with which he sought to draw Geneva back into the arms of the church, promising that the church would receive her as a compassionate mother receives a wandering daughter. Calvin's answer was most opportune, for Geneva had no pastor competent to answer Sadolet, who was "gifted with marvelous power and grace."

Calvin's answer was published and had a wide circulation; Luther was pleased, he said it was an answer which had both hands and feet.

The confusion bordering on anarchy that prevailed in Geneva, together with Calvin's powerful paper, induced the council to send a deputation to him, begging in the name of the council that he would return to Geneva, in order that the honor and glory of God might be promoted.

Calvin asked of the deputation, how the men who had banished him because of the strictness of his religious rule, could expect in the future to accommodate themselves to him, for he would not relax an iota of the strictness of his requirements. In reply, the council sent another deputation, offering such pressing and honorable terms, that Calvin promised to consider the matter. He was in no hurry to return, the council had not revoked the sentence of banishment against him, but in the following spring, 1541, the council solemnly revoked the sentence of banishment against Calvin, which they had pronounced three years before.

In August Calvin returned to Geneva, and for the remainder of his life the history of Geneva and the history of Calvin are linked into one. "Henceforth Calvin belonged to Geneva, and Geneva to Calvin."

CHAPTER XXIV.
JOHN CALVIN.

THE incoming New Year found Calvin's governmental arrangements, civil and ecclesiastical, all completed. The great and lesser councils, as heretofore, were the supreme civil tribunals; to these he added the consistory, the supreme spiritual tribunal. The consistory was composed of the city pastors and twelve laymen, recommended by the pastors and appointed by the councils. All matters pertaining to the church and the clergy, were to be considered and settled by this tribunal.

"The sign of the cross," said Calvin, "has been so grossly abused that it but serves to veil the absence of that which it signifies." He would not, therefore, allow the cross to be placed on the churches, but over the church doors he had inscribed the sacred letters, IHS, and he petitioned the council to pass the decree that the monogram of Christ should be inscribed on the public buildings, on the standards and on the coins of the city. Into church worship, Calvin introduced the "service of song," psalms in metre, printed with simple musical notation for congregational singing.

For many years the theocratic government established by Calvin moved on peacefully; there were occasional murmurs against his strictness of religious requirements, but there was no case of special severity and no open antagonism. The city was prosperous at home and respected abroad. It was the opinion of Michelet that "Geneva endured by her moral strength; she had no territory, no army, nothing for space, time or matter; she was the city of the mind, built of

Stoicism on the rock of Predestination." But as time wore on the struggle began, the tendency to social amusements, so long repressed, at last burst forth. Contrary to the ordinances Mrs. Perrin, wife of Amied Perrin, a man of high repute, gave a ball—had in her house music and dancing. She was indicted to appear before the consistory. She obeyed the indictment, but would not profess sorrow for what she had done nor would she promise not to do the like again; on the contrary, she was indignant against the consistory and gave them a piece of her mind on their usurpations. The consistory passed sentence of imprisonment on her and she was conveyed to prison. Her husband, who had been a friend of Calvin's, had left the city that he might not be compelled to witness against her. Calvin wrote to him, urging him to return and submit himself to the consistory. He returned—and was imprisoned. The imprisonment of Mr. and Mrs. Perrin is stated by some authorities to have been of several months' duration; by others, that it was a brief imprisonment of a few days. It was the beginning of serious troubles. A party was formed in Geneva, known as the Liberals; this party was hostile to Calvin, and between his party and the Liberals tumults and fights frequently occurred. Calvin, was sorely disturbed but he was inflexible, though menaces were uttered against all the pastors, and particularly against him. In this state of affairs, a crowd of angry, threatening men gathered in the hall of the Hotel de Ville to decide what steps they should take against their oppressors. Calvin was informed of the gathering by his alarmed brethren; he went straightway to the hotel and walked into their midst cool and impassive. "Citizens of Geneva," he said, "I know that I am the primary cause of all this confusion. If you will have blood, shed mine; if you wish me to be exiled, I will exile myself, and if you wish to try once more to save Geneva without the gospel, when I have exiled myself, you can try it." This bold attitude surprised and awed those who saw and heard him and produced a calm which seemed rapidly to spread over the city, but it was only on the surface; soon other conflicts arose between the two parties, and every conflict fanned the flame of discord. Many of Calvin's friends went over to the Liberals and at one time he thought that sentence of banishment would again be passed against him, but his influence proved to be the dominating power in Geneva.

In the year 1554—added to the civil and religious disturbances in the city—Geneva became the scene of the distressing imprisonment, unfair trial and cruel execution of Michael Servetus. Michael Servetus was born in Spain in 1509, and while yet a youth he was so much attracted by the reformed doctrine that his father sent him from Spain to France, fearing that the suspicion of the inquisitors might fall on the family. In France, where notwithstanding persecution the reformation had gained a firm foothold, Servetus allied himself with the movement. He is described as generous and courageous, as gifted and daring. Seeking knowledge from every available source, he studied medicine, law and divinity. "He toiled laboriously, and like a true son of the sixteenth century, he pried into everything." Servetus was haunted by the idea that "the reformers had stopped too soon, that Christianity, in order to become true again, needed a restoration deeper and far more complete." In order to give a clear exposition of his views, he wrote and published a work, for which he was apprehended and imprisoned in Vienne, but he managed to escape and fled to Geneva. On being informed of his presence in the city, Calvin demanded his arrest, which was ordered by the majority of the council. Into the audience chamber of the criminal court, situated in the prison, Servetus was conducted to answer to the charges contained in the articles, which had been drawn up by Calvin. The chief charges were pantheism and denial of the Trinity. Servetus asked for a public disputation with Calvin on the articles brought against him. His request was refused. On the following day Calvin was present and took part in the examination, which at times took the form of a disputation between the accused and the accuser. There was a proposition offered in the court to send to Vienne for a copy of the proceedings against Servetus in that court. Calvin objected to the proposition. He thought such a step might induce Berne and Basle to make an effort to save Servetus, as they had counseled clemency to Bolsec when he was under trial for holding opinions on some points, especially on predestination, opposed to the Genevan theology. Servetus had some few friends in the council—Amied Perrin was then a member of the council—but they formed so small a minority their voice had no controlling influence in the council.

The council and the consistory decreed death to the heretic. The day of his execution was set on the 27th of October, 1554, but for three months longer he was immured in a miserable dungeon. Servetus was under the impression that he was to die by the sword, but on his death-day when brought out from his loathsome dungeon and informed that he was to die by being burned at the stake, he threw himself prostrate before his judges, beseeching them to permit him to die by the sword, but his horror-struck supplication availed not with his judges. But they offered him life and liberty if he would retract his heresies, but his terror of the stake could not make him hesitate between truth and falsehood as he conceived them.

Calvin had withdrawn himself from the heretic; he had no word of kindness for his brother man in that man's hour of dire extremity.

The stake of Servetus excites the greater horror, the intenser shock, because it was planted by reformers in a reformed city. The burning at the stake of a man on account of his religious belief, no matter how clogged with error, by a consistory of reformed divines, and a council of reformed laymen, having in their hands the open gospel of him who said, "Blessed are the merciful," is more reprehensible, more criminal, than the burnings of unreformed Rome.

As prime mover in the death of Servetus, the lurid glare from that fatal pile will ever cast its shadow on the fair fame of Calvin. But all the blame cannot justly be thrown on him; before the sentence of death was passed the leading churches of Switzerland and of Germany were consulted, from not one of them came the voice of protest. Luther was no longer at the side of Melanchthon and he had not the courage to take his stand against the churches and say in the words of his Master, "Nay, let the wheat and the tares grow together until the harvest."

During the next year, the disturbances reached a crisis, the contending parties took up arms, and the Liberals, being the weaker party, were overcome; some of the prisoners escaped, others were executed, and all of that party were banished from the city.

The health of Calvin, never strong, began to give way some few years after the expulsion of the Liberals, and from the New Year of 1564, he was not again able to leave his house; near Whitsuntide of that year he closed his eyes in death. His remains were followed to the grave by a long procession of all the pastors of reformed Switzerland, and many from Germany and from France; the citizens of Geneva and many strangers were in the sad procession. A contemporary writes, "The church of Geneva bewailed the loss of her guide, and the state mourned for her chief citizen, her main protector after God."

As professor, as pastor and preacher, as writer and public adviser, Calvin was untiring. Besides his chief work, "Christian Institutes," and his commentaries on the Bible, his other works theological and polemical form quite a library. As a reformer he was earnest and courageous, and his example has been an inspiration to thousands.

CHAPTER XXV.

Reform Movement in France.

THE reform movement in France did not, at first, concern itself with doctrinal issues, it mainly strove to correct moral abuses and insist upon deeper spirituality, and this was done in isolated congregations, without any concerted action. Calvin, as a Frenchman and as a reformer, whose first pastorate had been in Paris, would naturally feel a deep interest in the cause of reform in France, and he did keep a watchful eye on the reform movement in that country.

Although the reform movement was so unaggressive, the reformers did not escape envious calumny. As a refutation of the charges laid against them, Calvin drew up and caused to be presented to the King of France, Henry II., "A Confession of Faith," in the name of the protestants of France, in order that the king might be truly informed of the faith of the abused people and therein see how false were the charges that had been spread against them. At the same time he urged upon the scattered congregations to unite in a regularly organized body. Calvin's opinion found favor with the reformed congregations and they resolved to send delegates to meet at the church in Paris and affect the desired organization.

The assembly met in the spring of 1559 in the small church of which Calvin had been pastor. It was a small gathering, not numbering fifty members, but it laid the foundation of the protestant church of France; it was entitled "The First National Synod of the Protestants of France." Being duly convened, the synod proceeded to draw up "A Confession of Faith." This work was readily accomplished because the protestants of France were of one mind in acceptance of Calvin's theology. The next work was to prepare a system of discipline, which should be also a constitution and of sufficient scope to become the basis of the additions which the future development of the church might demand. According to the definition of that synod, "The church, in the apostolic sense, is a body of believers assembled in one place for divine worship." And the synod enjoined upon every such church that, as soon as they could possibly do so, they should form themselves into a regularly organized body by appointing a consistory, by calling a pastor and by having regular preaching, and thereafter to bring together the several local churches into a general church; all the local churches in the same section of the country should send delegates—the pastor and one of the elders—to meet in conference semi-annually at some duly appointed place in order to consider the interests of the churches and to advise thereupon. As many of these conferences as could conveniently meet together annually should form a provincial synod to consider and control church affairs in the represented province; an important duty of this body was to appoint the pastors, subject to ratification by the churches. The supreme body of the church, the national synod, should consist of two pastors and two elders from each provincial synod. All questions of doctrines and general polity were to be submitted to this supreme body, and from its decisions no appeal could be taken.

The work of the "First National Synod," was unanimously approved by the churches. This well-arranged organization gave to the protestants of France, unity and strength. The subsequent rapid growth of protestantism is surprising; instead of a few hundreds, the protestant church of France increased to thousands and tens of thousands; she gathered in her membership from all ranks of society, from the humblest to the highest. Among her communicants were the Prince of Condé and Admiral Coligny, the Duchess of Ferrara and the Queen of Navarre.

In less than three years the Reformed church became so numerous and powerful that King Henry deemed it expedient to convoke the famous conference of Poissy, hoping that through the influence of the conference he might establish harmonious relations between the church of Rome and the Reformed church. In the conference both churches were represented by able men; Geneva had sent Theodore Beza. After his first speech, the Cardinal of Lorraine—brother of the Duke of Guise—declared that he wished the man had been dumb or that his hearers had been deaf. The representatives of Rome at Poissy affected to regard the Reformed church as a criminal; some of the prelates declared they were only there as her judges.

The conference of Poissy only disclosed more fully the then unbridgeable chasm between the two churches. The conference closed without an approach to the object the king had in view, but it was fruitful in good to the Reformed church. The masterly setting forth of the scriptural purity of the reformed doctrines and the primitive simplicity of worship had great influence upon large numbers of the people. Hundreds of parishes put down the mass, and numbers of priests became protestant pastors.

After the death of the king—under the regency of the Duke of Guise—the queen mother requested Admiral Coligny to give her a list of the Protestant churches already organized. The admiral found two thousand one hundred and fifty. The queen mother was restive under the power of the Guises, who under the pretence of extreme courtesy kept her in the background of political affairs, which was not at all to her liking. This state of affairs induced her to write to the Prince of Condé of a partially formed purpose of placing herself, the young king and kingdom under the protection of the protestants. She was weary of the Guises, and they were the head of the Romish church in France.

The cardinal was a much abler man than his brother, the duke. This was so well known in Paris that it was a common saying that the regent was the arm by which the cardinal worked the wires of state.

The young king, as dauphin, had been betrothed to Mary of Scots, who was then a child of five years old. Her uncles, the Guises, by their shrewd diplomacy, had succeeded in having the child-queen sent to France to be brought up and educated under their direction.

Before the ratification of the marriage, the duke and cardinal entered into a secret treaty with their niece by which the young queen bound herself to do all that in her power lay to bring her kingdom back into the church of Rome.

The young king, Francis II., had granted to the protestants the protection of a royal edict, known as the edict of January, but Francis was a weak man, physically and mentally. He passionately admired his beautiful wife and was ruled by her will, and she was controlled by the Guises, who continued to guide the helm of the ship of state as they had done when the king was a child. And under their continued rule the condition of the country seemed calm and prosperous. The protestants, with a sense of safety under the royal edict, were laboring for the promulgation of the gospel and for the good of the country, when suddenly, without premonition, the dark cloud of war was seen lowering in the near distance. The Guises, thirsting for protestant blood, had been plotting with foreign powers to invade France and help them to exterminate the heretics.

The armies of Spain and of Savoy marched into France and menaced the Prince of Condé in Orleans. In this exigency he appealed to protestant Germany and to protestant Switzerland for aid, and eagerly those protestant countries responded to his call, but the forces of the prince were far outnumbered by those of the enemy. In the battle of Dreux the protestants were defeated and the gallant Prince of Condé was taken prisoner.

All protestant France was sorely cast down: in this trying time Calvin wrote to the stricken church, "Since the poor flock of the Son of God has been scattered by the wolves, cling closer to Him and pray God to take pity on you, and stretch out His hand to shut their bloody mouths or turn them into lambs."

Though cast down and afflicted, the protestant church of France was still sufficiently powerful to command recognition as a church, co-existent with the church of Rome. It is said the king felt keenly the shame of his edict having been set aside as a nullity. In the spring of the next year, 1564, he issued another edict known as the edict of Amboise, which was thankfully received by the oppressed protestants, though it was less favorable than the edict of January. Notwithstanding the king's edict, the protestant church was the object of continuous envy and persecution all through the eight years that led to the fatal day of St. Bartholomew. On that day of horror, the noble Coligny perished. That massacre of innocent and unsuspecting people was planned and guided by the Guises.

Henceforth the history of the protestant church of France is one of perils and persecutions until Henry of Navarre was crowned Henry IV. of France. He issued the edict of Nantes, which secured to the oppressed and persecuted church, both political and religious liberty, and again she became a flourishing and powerful body. But, alas! her prosperity was short-lived. Monarchical despotism culminated under Louis XIV.; in 1685 he revoked the edict of Nantes; that revocation was the death blow of the protestant church of France.

CHAPTER XXVI.

ENGLISH REFORMATION.

The reformation in England did not grow out of the rupture between Henry VIII. and the pope; the only effect that rupture had upon the English reformation was to throw the royal authority on the side of the reform movement. The temporal authority in Saxony and in the Swiss reformed cantons from the first was on the side of reform and from nobler motives than actuated Henry VIII. of England.

The germ of the English reformation must be sought far back in the teachings of Robert Greathead and of his spiritual son, John Wycliffe, and in the teachings of many others, their successors.

By some authorities it is claimed that the first impulse toward the great reformation of the sixteenth century in England was given by Cardinal Wolsey. He certainly gave a renewed impetus to the study of Greek, and he enlarged the university libraries, and demanded a better educated clergy; and further, he suppressed the smaller monasteries by placing the inmates of several in one monastery to be supported by its revenues. Of the vacated monasteries, some were converted into bishoprics and others into colleges. And it is claimed that by original documents, it can be proven that he handled the large revenues thus freed from monastic control with clean hands, appropriating them to schools, colleges and other public needs. The degradation of Cardinal Wolsey from power, it is claimed, was not so much owing to the cupidity of the king as to his desire to crush so powerful an opponent of his will in the divorce from Queen Catharine. Shakespeare makes Wolsey say:

"I have touched the highest point of all my greatness,
And from that full meridian of my glory,
I haste now to my setting."

That hasted setting leaves in darkness whatever of civil and religious reform might have been gained under Cardinal Wolsey. But it is clear as noonday that the desire for civil and religious reform was not the moving principle with Wolsey's king; he was actuated by a two-fold motive, resentment against the pope and acquisition of wealth and power. His suppression of the monasteries was not for the sake of religious reform nor for the public weal, but to destroy an adverse power; a power behind the throne devoted to Rome and by all possible means working against him as supreme head of the English church. And, moreover, the confiscation of their immense riches would be a fountain of wealth to his attenuated treasury. But without cloaking his purpose under the pretense of religious reform and the public weal, he could not, in freedom-loving England, have accomplished a dissolution of the monasteries by the sole exercise of his royal power.

For more than a century there had been a growing sentiment among the secular clergy and among the people, that the monastic system, decrepit with age and bloated with wealth, was a plague-spot on the realm; it was this growing public sentiment that influenced the action of Cardinal Wolsey.

The dissolution of the monasteries was unquestionably both a civil and a religious blessing. The useless lives and the general wickedness of the monks made them an offence to the moral sense of the better class of the people, and a stumbling block in the path of religious reform. At the same time there were many individual exceptions, noble men, of holy and useful lives; and in many instances the course pursued by the king and his minister, Cromwell, was altogether reprehensible. They cannot be exonerated from the charges of rapacity and cruelty upon testimony that was not substantiated. Venerable and worthy abbots were condemned and executed, and monks who were devout and scholarly had to share the same fate. Books were wantonly defaced and destroyed; cartloads of them were burned.

The king's greed of gold and of power was not exceeded by his greed of blood; both are dark stains on his character.

The monastic property, in jewels and plate, in money and in estates, confiscated by the king, is recorded to have amounted to over fifty millions of pounds sterling; of this vast amount, only about one million was expended for the public good. Dr. Cranmer, archbishop of Canterbury, prevailed upon the king to pension the aged and infirm monks and nuns, and to convert many of the monasteries into schools and colleges to be supported out of the revenues that pertained to the monasteries. Bishop Latimer petitioned the king to preserve in each county one monastery, to be set apart as a place of retirement for aged scholars, and of resort for studious younger men; for its support, he prayed that the amount needed should be secured to it out of the property which had belonged to that monastery.

After the pensions, endowments and bequests were granted, the sharp watchfulness of the king could not prevent a considerable portion of the large wealth from passing into private channels. The suspicions of the king were strongly aroused against Lord Cromwell, of having made large personal appropriations to himself, over and above the seven rich priories which had been assigned to him.

In parliament and in church convocations, measures were taken to complete the separation of the church of England from the church of Rome, and to establish the royal supremacy over the church of England. The final step was taken by the parliament of 1534, which passed the act giving to the sovereign of England the title, "Supreme Head, under Christ, of the Church of England." And the same parliament placed in the hands of the archbishop of Canterbury the spiritual jurisdiction of the church of England. Two years after Archbishop Cranmer called a convocation of the clergy, for the purpose of reforming the doctrines and regulating the services of the church. Lord Cromwell was presented to the convocation as the king's vicar general; he brought the greeting of their royal head and declared his majesty's desire, that the action of the convocation might happily terminate all religious discord.

As a basis of doctrine, the convocation prepared and published the Ten Articles, the first of a series of articles which concluded with the "Thirty-nine Articles," the confession of faith of the church of England.

Of the ten articles, the first five treated of doctrines; the last five of rites and ceremonies; and the convocation decreed that in the future all the services of the sanctuary should be conducted in the English tongue. To have the Bible in the native tongue had, from the first, been a dear wish of the English heart, as witness Bede, Alfred, Wycliffe, and others. And at this convocation, Archbishop Cranmer proposed to the bishops that by their united labor they should give the Bible to the English people in the English tongue. In his speech he tells them, "It is not much above a hundred years since the scripture hath ceased to be read in the vulgar tongue within this realm, but our language hath so changed, that the former translations cannot be well understood by the people; it therefore behooves us to set about the work of translation." That hundred years and more of which the archbishop spoke had shut off the knowledge of the Bible from the masses of the people; nevertheless, the archbishop's proposition met with decided opposition among the bishops, some among them declaring that it is not necessary, that it is not best, that the scripture be in the English tongue and in the hands of the common people. And for the time the proposition was overruled. But true to his purpose, the archbishop and those bishops friendly to the measure, set about the work and accomplished it; and under royal license, the Great Bible was published before the close of the year 1537. The royal sanction was readily given to place the Great Bible in the churches, to be read and expounded to the edification of the people, and the privilege of private ownership was further granted, but only the better class of the people were able to avail themselves of the privilege.

More than twelve years before the publication of the Great Bible, the spirit of William Tyndale, an earnest reformer and a learned man, had been stirred within him because the scriptures were not in the native tongue of the people, especially the New Testament; and he set to work to translate the New Testament into English. He declared that his heart's desire was "that a copy of the New Testament might be in the hands of every plough-boy in England." The book was published at Antwerp in 1526 and sent over to England; many of the clergy were bitterly opposed to its general circulation; one bishop bought up a whole edition to prevent its circulation among the people, but that and other like measures failed to keep the book from the people who were eager to get it. A party of the bishops finding that strategy was of no avail called an episcopal convention that they might take measures to prevent the New Testament in the vulgar tongue from falling into the hands of the unlearned, who could not understand it. The convention condemned the book to be burned wherever it was found, but Archbishop Cranmer, who had opposed the action of the convention, induced the king to declare its condemnation of the book to be a sentence null and void.

The gladness of the people at having the New Testament in their own familiar speech may have been a chief means of deciding the archbishop to put the whole Bible into English and to place it in the churches to be read for the instruction of the people.

CHAPTER XXVII.

THE ENGLISH CHURCH.

HENRY VIII. died in 1554; his son and successor, Edward VI., was but nine years old; but, young as he was, such were the graces of his mind and manner, he was called "a marvelous boy." Bishop Burnet says of him, "He had great understanding, being capable of comprehending whatever was laid before him, and from the first had a liking to all good and generous principles." During the minority of the young king, his uncle, the Duke of Somerset, was appointed regent or protector. The duke was a moderate reformer; all his measures favored the reform movement, and he was a good man, but not a sagacious ruler. He excited the jealousy of the nobles by an over-reach of power and the displeasure of the nation by involving the country in an unprofitable foreign war. But in adversity his character shows to advantage; when he was deprived of power and thrown into prison by the accusing nobles he employed his time as a Christian philosopher; and on his partial restoration to power he showed Christian leniency towards his enemies. The early years of Edward's reign are memorable for measures of pacific conservatism. The Duke of Somerset, holding the reins of government in his hands, induced the first parliament under Edward VI. to pass an act against all rash innovations, under penalty of imprisonment; all the measures of the duke were moderate, but the zeal of the young king was more active in the cause of reform. When but a boy of twelve years he wrote out a plan for the right furtherance of the reformation to its purposed end, the establishment of true and undefiled religion in the realm of

England. He was a warm admirer of Calvin, who had dedicated to him two books, and had written him several letters of commendation and advice; Edward often said he was pleased and profited both by the books and the letters. His young mind soon acquired a bent toward Genevan theology and toward Genevan plainness in the form of worship, a severe plainness which would not tolerate even a cross on the churches. The teachings of Calvin exercised considerable influence over both the laity and the clergy of the reformed church of England. That influence was the mother of English puritanism.

Mere boy as was King Edward VI., such was the superiority of his mental powers and the strength of his will that during the last three years of his reign he was not only a king in name, he was a king in reality; he did not hesitate to thrust his pen through any act either of parliament or of convocation that did not impress him as being for the good of the people or of the church.

Under his royal influence, parliament passed an act abolishing the mass and by another act made the administration of the Lord's Supper in both kinds to all communicants, the law of the land, and yet another, that all pictures and images should be removed from the churches. King Edward ordered that the raiment on the images should be given to the poor. He held the opinion that, if for no other cause, the removal of the statues from the churches was necessary in order to prevent the living images of Christ from quarreling about the lifeless ones.

Under acts of parliament confession was no longer obligatory, and the right of marriage was granted to the clergy. About this time, in obedience to a royal edict, a full convocation met in Canterbury, both the upper house and the lower having full representation. The purpose of the convocation was to set forth more clearly the doctrines of the reformed church of England and to establish her liturgy. A large amount of work was accomplished by the convocation, but the most important work was the elaboration of the Ten Articles—under Henry VIII.—into forty-two articles. Under Queen Elizabeth the forty-two articles were reduced to thirty-nine, which, from that time to this, have continued to be the "Articles of Faith," in the Protestant Episcopal church. The bringing forth in its entirety of the Book of Common Prayer, known as the Prayer Book of Edward VI., was another important work of the convocation. This book established the liturgy of the church of England. Though by the work of the convocation the liturgy of the church was confirmed and settled, the question of vestments continued to disquiet both the civil and the clerical mind. Many, among the laity and among the clergy, had received, as seed sown in good soil, the teachings of Bucer—who then held a professorship in England—on needful simplicity in clerical costume; but the case of Dr. Hooper, bishop elect of Gloucester, finally settled the question of vestments, at least so far as the clergy were concerned. Dr. Hooper, at his consecration, or rather at the time set for his consecration, refused to put on the episcopal vestments, stating as the ground of his refusal that they were not in keeping with the simplicity of the Christian religion; that they were brought into the church for the purpose of celebrating mass with greater pomp, and had been handed down through the force of tradition. The consecration was postponed, and the matter referred by the king to his beloved and honored instructor, Archbishop Cranmer—into whose hands, by act of parliament and by royal sanction, the spiritual jurisdiction of the church of England had been placed. The archbishop called a convention of bishops and submitted the matter to their joint consideration. Bishops Ridley and Latimer declared in the name of the body, that tradition should be rejected in matters of faith, but might be accepted concerning rites and ceremonies, and the archbishop decided that while the law of the land sanctioned the use of vestments, it was the duty of the clergy to wear them, and equally the duty of bishops to wear the episcopal vestments. And Bishop Hooper, as a law-abiding citizen, consented to receive consecration in episcopal vestments; and his act rejoiced the heart of the young king, for it restored the harmony of faith and action in the church he loved so well. The enactments known as the "Laws of King Edward" threw around the reformed church all necessary safeguards, but they were subsequently set at naught by time-serving parliaments and the bloody hand of power. It is sadly surprising to find the parliaments of the sixteenth century so subservient to the sovereign, no matter whether protestant or papist.

Sad was the day for England when young Edward died, and sadder still was the day when Mary ascended the throne; sad and bloody were the years of her reign.

Bishop Burnet states that her father, Henry VIII., provoked at her obstinacy and impatient of her contradiction to his royal will, had determined to strike terror into all who might dare to oppose him by having her put to death; not one of the nobles or bishops who favored her faith would so far venture his own interest, or hazard his life, as to appeal to the king on her behalf. Archbishop Cranmer was the only one who dared to stand forth in her cause; he entreated the king for her, he pleaded with him not to forget that he was a father, and not to proceed to extremity against his young daughter. The archbishop besought the king not even to blame her too severely for her obstinate adherence to that form of religion which she had learned from her mother and from all who had surrounded her. And the good archbishop wisely urged upon the king that such an act would excite the horror of all Europe against himself. Archbishop Cranmer saved Mary from the headsman's axe; she sent him to the burning stake.

After her coronation Mary desired to take such steps immediately as would restore the union between England and the Roman church, but her party leaders saw the danger attendant upon precipitate action, and counselled prudence, or her government might be overthrown without consideration of queen or pope.

Notwithstanding the talk of lawful proceedings, under royal favor measures were carried through without law; the images were replaced in the churches, papal rites and ceremonies were re-established, together with the Latin service and the mass. The things that were abolished under law were restored without law. But no death sentence for heresy was passed until after the marriage of the queen with her cousin, Philip of Spain. The united influence of Philip, Cardinal Pole, and the queen's confessor, a Spanish Dominican monk, aroused and brought into action the bigotry and cruelty of her Spanish blood.

On the charges of sedition and of heresy a large number of protestants were arrested, thrown into prison, tried and condemned as obstinate heretics. The blood of the martyrs began to flow, and before the close of Mary's reign two hundred and fifty-one protestants of the laity, men and women, and twenty-six of the clergy, endured the terrible death of burning at the stake, because they would not abjure their faith. The archbishops of Canterbury and of York, and Bishops Ridley, Latimer and Hooper were arrested and cast into prison. The life of protestants being hourly in danger, more than a thousand of them fled to the continent, and under protestant protection, remained in voluntary exile until after the death of the bloody queen.

On the meeting of the next parliament Dr. Taylor, bishop of Lincoln, and Dr. Harley, bishop of Hereford, determined to present themselves in the house of lords to justify their doctrine and insist upon protestant rights under the existing law of King Edward. They felt called to this duty, as the heads of the reformed church were in prison on the charge of treason and of sedition. The two bishops presented themselves in the house of lords in their episcopal robes, but they refused to do reverence at the opening service of the mass, which excited a tumult in the house, and they were violently thrust out and were not again permitted to enter. It lay not in their power to extend other than spiritual help to their brethren.

Some sixteen bishoprics and twelve thousand benefices were conferred upon papal aspirants. Mary and her Spanish husband resolved to do all in their power, by law when they could command a compliant parliament, and without law when they could not, to lay England at the feet of the pope.

To the papal party and to the queen, the Princess Elizabeth was an object of fear and jealousy; a charge of disloyalty was concocted and brought against her; she was arrested and sent a prisoner to the Tower, and treated with such severity that her health failed under it. The queen feared to push her power to extremity and the princess was removed to Hatfield, and the severity of her treatment so relaxed, that it was but partial imprisonment, but she was surrounded by spies, eager to seize upon any suspicious word or deed. The princess being aware of the fact, refrained from all participation in outer affairs and gave her time to study.

During the imprisonment of Bishop Ridley and Bishop Latimer, many efforts were made to induce them to recant, promises of royal favor were held out to them, but all to no purpose; they stood unmoved, rooted and grounded in the faith as it is in Christ. They were declared obstinate heretics and sentenced to the stake. In the city of Oxford on the sixteenth day of October, 1555, these faithful ministers of the Word of God were led to the place of execution, on the south front of Balliol College; at the stake they embraced each other, Bishop Ridley saying, "Be of good heart, brother, God will either assuage the fury of the flames or enable us to abide it." Bishop Ridley was a man of profound learning and sound judgment, and ranks as the ablest man of the English reformation; Bishop Latimer, though less learned, was a pattern of piety and Christian simplicity, a father in his diocese and a leader in the English reformation.

Archbishop Cranmer had been also removed to Oxford, many arguments had been presented to him, which he had refuted, and many inducements which he had withstood, but alas for the weakness of the flesh! at last, he signed his name to the papers of recantation, which were drawn up and brought to him in his prison. But when the set day came, on which he was to declare his recantation, his conversion to the church of Rome, in deep contrition of spirit, he declared that in all his life there was nothing he so deeply deplored as he did the setting of his hand to those papers. And there, standing face to face with death, in one of its most horrible forms, he rejected the supremacy of the pope and acknowledged the scripture as his highest law. On the south front of Balliol College, Archbishop Cranmer was burned at the stake. He met his end as a brave Christian, his weakness was gone. As the flames surged upwards, he held out his right hand saying, "This unworthy right hand," and as the flames rose higher, he cried with Stephen, "Lord Jesus receive my spirit," and so passed away from earth. Two days after his death Cardinal Pole was consecrated Archbishop of Canterbury.

Though the flames consumed the bodies of the martyrs, they could not destroy the love of the reformed religion in the hearts of the survivors. Those who loved the simplicity of the gospel of Christ, with caution and secrecy met often together under the care of faithful shepherds willing to risk their lives in order to feed the flocks committed to their care.

Queen Mary died on the morning of the seventeenth of November, 1558, and as the sovereign never dies, Elizabeth was in a few hours proclaimed queen, and on the proclamation a great shout went up from the people, "God save Queen Elizabeth, long and happy be her reign!" The funeral obsequies and the interment of the late queen were conducted with all the usual honors of royalty, though few sad faces were seen, save those of the papal priests and bishops, "who were forced to betake themselves to secret groans, since they durst not vent them in public." Shortly afterward the confessor of the late queen and most of the Spaniards and Italians fled from the country. When the news of Queen Mary's death reached France, the cardinal of Lorraine endeavored to induce the pope to declare Elizabeth illegitimate and Mary of Scotland the rightful heir to the crown of England, but Pope Paul IV. seemed not inclined to move in the matter.

CHAPTER XXVIII.
Queen Elizabeth.

On her accession, Queen Elizabeth issued a proclamation that no breach, alteration, or change should be allowed of any order or usage established in the realm. Her opening policy was conservative, as had been the policy of the first years of the reign of her brother Edward.

The coronation of the queen was not until after the New Year. She was crowned at Westminster Abbey, "with all the magnificence attending the coronation of illustrious sovereigns."

On her way to the abbey, as the queen drove under one of the triumphal arches erected for the occasion, an elegantly bound Bible was let down to her by a child who stood on the arch, representing Truth; the queen received the book with reverence, and humbly kissing the sacred volume declared that it pleased her more than any other of the offerings of the day.

The queen began her long reign with wise moderation, she continued several of the officers of state who were papists, but her chief advisers were Sir Robert Cecil, afterward Lord Burleigh, and Sir Nicholas Bacon, both staunch protestants. In was the opinion of these ministers that a certain measure of consideration was due from the queen to all her subjects, and that such a course would prove the surest way of uniting the people in one faith and in one form of worship.

A royal mandate was issued ordering that all who had been imprisoned on account of their religious belief should be set at liberty; but a general questioning arose, "When will the queen begin to restore the former purity of the church?" To this question the answer was given, "At the next parliament."

The first parliament under the reign of Queen Elizabeth met in January, 1559, and sat until May. The first act placed upon the statute book of that memorable parliament was an act to re-establish the independence of the Church of England. The Book of Common Prayer was restored to the churches under a new act of uniformity, and other measures were enacted of high importance. After these acts of parliament, some of the English papal clergy gave in their adhesion to the established church, some retired to private life and others went over to France. The news of this orderly and successful launching of the English Ship of State and Church was unwelcome news at Rome, and Pius IV., successor to Paul IV., wrote a long, loving letter to the queen, urging her to return to the bosom of the church for the salvation of her own soul and of her whole nation. Such a step, he assures her, "will fill the universal church with rejoicing and gladness, yea, you shall make glad heaven itself, and encircle your brow with a glory far exceeding that of the crown you wear." The pope sent his letter by a confidential agent, who was authorized to press upon the queen every possible conciliatory measure. With a few changes the agent was to accept the English Prayer Book, to permit service in the vulgar tongue, and to proffer to herself the most flattering personal promises. But to all these Queen Elizabeth turned a deaf ear.

The pope finding that flattery and promises of increased power availed naught with the Queen of England, issued against her a bull of excommunication, and by fraud and force he labored to bring about her destruction. He tried to excite rebellion among English Catholics, and at the same time he endeavored to induce the King of Spain to make war upon England and conquer the country for himself, promising to bestow the papal sanction on his sovereignty. But the pope's fair-seeming and foul-scheming were alike bootless.

Pope Pius V. endeavored through Mary Queen of Scots, then held in durance in England, to subvert the government, assassinate the queen, destroy the Church of England, and bring the country under the papal yoke. Into this plot the Cardinal of Lorraine and the Duke of Guise threw the whole force of their influence. An Italian merchant residing in England was appointed secret papal nuncio and commissioned to form a secret league of English and Scotch catholics; this league was to circulate among the people a papal bull, excommunicating the queen and all who should thereafter yield her obedience. The pope's bull deprived her of her kingdom and freed her subjects from their oaths of allegiance; and further, commanded all English subjects to acknowledge Mary of Scotland as queen of England.

These papal measures were pushed so strenuously that the northern rebellion was soon organized and waiting further orders. The duke of Norfolk was chosen commander, and the necessary money supplies were remitted by the pope, and with her own consent the pope had promised to bestow upon the duke of Norfolk the hand of queen Mary, whom he pronounced to be Queen of Scotland and of England. While these things were being done in England, the pope, backed by the Cardinal of Lorraine, "did manage dexterously with the court of France, in order to its favoring the Catholics of England." The pope also goaded the king of Spain to send an invading army into England from Flanders, to which country he sent "a great supply of money."

Never was so far reaching a plot more sagaciously laid, nor its details carried out with greater secrecy. The simultaneous uprising in the north of England, the landing of a strong detachment of the Spanish army in the southeast, and the burning of all the shipping on the Thames, must have overpowered protestant England, and sounded the death knell of her established church had she been unsuspecting and unprepared, as the pope so fondly hoped and so fully believed her to be. But England was not resting unsuspectingly at her ease, she knew the enemies with whom she had to deal. Lord Burleigh maintained efficient agents in Italy, who, by freely using "the silver key," gained access to the secrets of the conspirators. From one of his agents Lord Burleigh received timely information of the conspiracy in all its details. "A list was forwarded to him of several consultations amongst the cardinals, bishops and others of the several orders of Rome, now a-contriving and conspiring against her gracious majesty and the established Church of England." This information put the English government on the alert and using all diligence many suspicious persons were arrested, among whom was the Duke of Norfolk. Shortly thereafter a man bound for Scotland was taken at the crossing of a river, he had concealed about him letters from the Duke of Norfolk and money to the value of a thousand pounds, money and letters to be delivered to certain Catholic nobles in Scotland, the letters notifying them to have their forces ready at a given time.

The Duke of Norfolk, his secretary and several others implicated in the treason were tried, condemned and executed before the pope's well laid plot had fully matured. Her gracious majesty and the established Church of England were saved through the wisdom and faithfulness of an agent in Italy, whose name was Denham; his "List" is preserved in manuscript in the British Museum.

Catena mentions with what excess of sorrow the pope lamented the failure of his well laid plans.

One other effort, the great and final effort to conquer England for the pope, was made in 1588. In May of that year Spain sent out her mighty fleet, to which the pope had given every aid which he could possibly render; under his special apostolic blessing the Spanish Armada sailed for England to destroy heresy in that island. But before the summer closed the great Armada was destroyed. The winds and the storms were the allies of the gallant British sailors in the destruction of the great invading fleet of Spain. This great victory was a prime means of assuring the perpetuity of the Reformation in England.

The enfranchisement of the human mind begun by the Renaissance and carried on to higher planes by the reformation in its fourfold development, justifies Pastor Bungener in saying that, "Humanly speaking, the reformation was the daughter of learning, and she has everywhere labored to secure the reign of knowledge; in doing this she but secures what is her own and thereby that which belongeth unto the gospel." Yea, through the continuous unfolding of the vital principles of the reformation, human nature will continue to develop a higher civilization and a deeper enthusiasm of humanity, and will attain unto a clearer apprehension of the sublime simplicity of the truth as it is in Jesus, and thereby grow unto the stature of sons and daughters of God, loyal to Truth, to Liberty and to Love.

PART IV.

CHAPTER XXIX.

GREAT MEN OF FLORENCE.

STATESMAN; ARTIST; PROPHET—PRIEST AND HISTORIAN.

In our strenuous age, abounding in mechanical inventions, in manifold industries, in continuously increasing wants, in the stress of business and in the whirl of society, the large majority of men and women cannot find the time to dig and delve in the mines of learning. And hence it behooves those who are urged on by the mandate of nature to find themselves in duty bound to share with their brethren the spoils they have won.

All those who believe that the highest study of man is man, feel a perennial interest in the leading events of the lives of men, particularly of men who have exerted a formative influence upon their times. Such men were Cosmo di Medici, and his grandson, the Great Lorenzo. Such men were the unique Artking, Michael Angelo, the prophet-priest Savonarola, and the concise historian Machiavelli.

These men helped forward the regeneration of letters, of religion and of art. And beautiful Florence, city of their birth, is well worthy of a brief consideration, for she was the cherishing mother of learning and of art, and she was the capital of the most renowned of the republics of Italy.

Even as the mighty oak grows from a small acorn, so the great city of Florence grew from a very small beginning, from a few warehouses built in the plain of the Arno for the convenience of the merchants of Fiesole, an ancient town on the summit of the mountain. In the wake of the warehouse followed homes for the traders, thereby saving both the time and labor which had been spent in climbing the mountain to reach their homes in Fiesole; soon streets were laid off and blocks of houses were built, and Florence grew into an important mercantile town. But this was the re-birth of a humble town said to have been founded by Charlemagne.

In his history of Florence, Machiavelli states that the town was destroyed by Totilla, king of the Ostrogoths, and that it lay in ruins for two hundred and fifty years. "It was," he says, "built by Charlemagne, but attained no distinction and did not greatly increase in numbers nor effect anything worthy of memory, being kept down by foreign rulers."

In 1215 Florence succeeded in establishing her liberty. After that time, says the historian of Florence, "it is scarcely possible to imagine the power and authority Florence in a short time acquired; she became not only the head of Tuscany, but one of the greatest cities of Italy."

And Florence led the van in the march of progression from mediæval to modern times.

"Where smiling Arno sweeps,
Was modern luxury and commerce born,
And buried learning rose redeemed to a new morn."

"Sad, visaged Dante," prince of Italian poets, was a native of Florence, and he loved his native city with passionate devotion. In the struggle between the citizens and the nobles, Dante, believing that true liberty was under the old empire, sided with the nobles and the emperor. To his poet mind the ideal was more real than the actual; his poetic enthusiasm led him to glorify the venerated past, and oppose the liberty for which the citizens were striving as subversive of the divine order of things.

The citizens succeeded in establishing republican liberty, and blindly banished their poet because his political views did not accord with their own. After his death they set up his statue for the honor of Florence. In his sonnet on Dante, Michael Angelo asks:

"How shall we speak of him? for our blind eyes
Are all unequal to his dazzling rays.
Easier it is to blame his enemies
Than it is to tell his meed of praise.
For he, great poet, did explore the realms of woe;
And at his coming high heaven did expand
Her lofty gates, to whom his native land
Refused to open hers."

Florence reached the acme of her glory under the rule of the di Medicis. And eventually, under unworthy descendants of the same family, she fell from her high estate. The proud and powerful republic of Florence was crushed under the heel of the later di Medicis, who made themselves princes and changed the republic into a principality.

The first of that famous family who attained political distinction was Salvestro di Medici; in 1378 he was elected governor of the city and chief magistrate of the republic. From the end of his term of office to the close of his life he was the leading citizen of Florence. The family did not belong to the ancient nobility, but stood first among the popular families. The ancient nobility had for more than a generation been restive under the growing influence of the di Medicis; in this only were they united, their contentions and quarrels among themselves not unfrequently led to public riots. When Giovanni di Medici was elected to the chief magistracy they strove to displace him, but he quietly held to the even tenor of his way and silenced all opposers. He loved peace and shunned war. He relieved his fellow citizens in adversity and protected them in prosperity. He never applied the public money to his own uses, but contributed of his private wealth to the public weal. "He died," says Machiavelli, "very rich in money, but more exceeding rich in good repute and in the best wishes of mankind, and his wealth and his great fame were preserved and increased by his son Cosmo, who succeeded him in the government."

But the enmity of the noble factions raged more fiercely against Cosmo than it had done against his father. The nobles agreed to bury their animosities against each other in order to combine against him and procure his banishment. They succeeded—Cosmo was sent into exile. He received his sentence without complaint, and assured the Signory—or Congress—that he would quietly remain in the place to which they had banished him. The people were despondent at the departure of a man so generally beloved, and it was not long before the Signory found out that they had made a great mistake; tumults and riots soon filled the city, "her condition was little short of anarchy." The Signory recalled Cosmo, and begged him to take again the reins of government. The return of Cosmo to the city which had banished him resembled the coming home of a conqueror on whose banners sat victory. As he approached the city he was met by a vast concourse of people, and with universal consent was hailed as "Father of His Country." And he ruled Florence long and wisely. He was the friend and patron of men of letters, and did much to advance the new learning. "When he died the republic of Florence and all Christian princes condoled with his son Piero." The funeral of Cosmo was conducted with the utmost pomp and solemnity. All classes of citizens followed his remains to the tomb in the church of San Lorenzo. By a public decree, on his tomb was inscribed: "Father of His Country." Piero succeeded to the government. His rule was mild; he did not very long survive his father. He left two sons, Lorenzo and Giuliano, who ruled conjointly. Lorenzo, though a young man, resolved that all public transactions should bear his impress; he was ambitious, but his ambition was tempered by prudence and wisdom.

The family of Pazzi was immensely rich and belonged to the ancient nobility. They considered themselves neglected in the distribution of public honors, both by the Signory and the di Medici, and they set about devising ways and means of vengeance. They sought out all who were opposed to the Medicis, not only in Florence but in Rome.

CHAPTER XXX.

Conspiracy against the di Medicis.

THE reigning pope, Sixtus IV., was a man of low origin and of lower nature, but by means of his talents he became general of the Order of St. Francis, then cardinal and finally pope. Machiavelli says: "Sixtus IV. was the first pope to show to the world how much that, which was previously regarded as sinful, lost its iniquity when committed by a pontiff." Sixtus IV. resolved to hold the territories of the church in obedience, and, as a fearful warning to the rebellious minded, he caused the city of Spoletto to be *sacked* because the people rebelled against his arbitrary authority. For the same cause he besieged Castello; the prince of Castello was the friend of Lorenzo di Medici, and in his hour of need he applied to Lorenzo for aid, and Lorenzo sent him the desired assistance. This act aroused the anger of the pope against the di Medicis and made him their bitter enemy. The plot to compass the death of the two brothers, Lorenzo and Giuliano, was hatched in Rome, headed by one of Pazzi brothers, who resided in Rome. Cardinal Riario, a protegé of the pope, and the Archbishop of Pisa were among the active conspirators, and the pope lent his aid by offering the papal troops. Emissaries were sent to Florence to sound Jacopo Pazzi, the father. He at first, from religious scruples, declined to join the conspiracy, but the pope soon removed all scruples, and he entered heartily into the plot and readily assisted in arranging the diabolical details. The papal troops were quartered by companies, so as not to arouse suspicion, in towns near to Florence, and it was shortly rumored through the city that Cardinal Riario would honor Florence with a visit.

CONSPIRACY AGAINST THE DI MEDICIS. 181

The Medicis were aware of the animosity of the Pazzi and of their desire to deprive them of the government, and were anticipating an open attempt on the part of the Pazzi to win over the civil authority, and, if possible, depose them; a conspiracy to assassinate them they did not suspect. The cardinal came with a large retinue, composed chiefly of conspirators. The Medicis were invited to call on the cardinal, and it was decided that as the brothers sat in the social group the assassins were to do their work, but the brothers went singly, and thus frustrated the diabolical purpose for that time.

As a last hope of getting them together it was determined that the assassination should take place in the cathedral during high mass. The brothers Pazzi had chosen to be the assassins, but on entering the church the elder Pazzi was awed by the place, and declared that he could not kill a man in that sacred edifice. Among the conspirators were two men to whom secret murder was no unusual thing— one of the men was a priest—they were nothing loth, for the largeness of the pay, to take the places of the Pazzi. The signal agreed upon was the first chime of the bell during mass.

The congregation assembled, but it was observed that Giuliano di Medici was absent. One of the Pazzi went to fetch him, and, with great show of kindness, sat beside him.

The solemn service began; the stroke of the bell fell upon unsuspecting ears, but instantly the sons of Belial struck their victims. Giuliano stepped forward, but the dagger of the Pazzi at his side struck him to the floor. Though the victim lay bleeding and wounded to the death, again and again Francesco Pazzi thrust his dagger in him. In his hellish greed of blood he unwittingly gave himself a wound, which proved his death wound. Lorenzo was in a distant part of the church; at the moment of the signal the assassin, who had been stationed near him, struck him on the neck with his dagger, but failing to touch a vital part, Lorenzo sprang up and bravely defended himself.

So suddenly had the diabolical scene transpired, that the congregation could not at first understand the cause of the tumult, but seeing Lorenzo attacked and fighting for his life, they rushed to him and bore him in their arms to the sacristy and secured the strong doors. The uproar in the church was terrible; the people in their rage rushed at the cardinal, but his followers pushed him close to the altar and surrounded and defended him; the assassin priest and his accomplice were slain on the chancel pavement. Without the Archbishop of Pisa, commanding a division of the papal troops marched to the palace of government.

The officers of government were required to live in the palace during their term of office. They were at dinner when they were startled by the noise below and by the clash of arms, but they did not lose their presence of mind; they snatched up such arms as could be readily obtained, and hastily gathering the armed servitors of the palace, they put themselves at their head and forced back the besieging troops, which were led by the archbishop and one of the Pazzi. Both of these commanders were caught, ropes were thrown around their necks, and they were pushed through the windows and there they hung; quite a large number of the soldiers were pitched through windows and falling on the pavement below, some were killed and others lay writhing, bruised and mangled by the fall. Part of the troops succeeded in forcing the doors of the ground floor and barricaded themselves there.

The great alarm bell was rung, the whole city heard the alarm, men hurriedly armed and soon the streets were thronged with armed citizens hurrying to the public square of the palace. They made short work with the papal troops, which had barricaded themselves in the lower story of the palace of government.

Not knowing the state of affairs, Jacopo Pazzi, old and infirm, rode forth with a hundred horsemen, to induce the people and the Signory to aid in destroying the Medici, and putting down all their adherents; his appeals and his promises were alike unheeded as he rode through the streets. When he reached the public square and saw the dead body of his son and that of the archbishop hanging from the windows of the palace, he knew the conspiracy was crushed; he turned his horse and fled to the country, his men following; he was pursued, captured, brought back, tried and executed within four days.

CHAPTER XXXI.

Lorenzo the Magnificent.

WHEN the news of the proceedings reached Rome, the pope raged in his anger; he hurled his bull of excommunication against Florence, and threatened the city with the Interdict. The people of Florence were indignant, and yet, alarmed at the dread prospect, fearless hearts quailed at the thought of the Interdict. The news of the death of the pope shortly after was welcome tidings to Florence. The new pope, Innocent VIII., was the friend and the relation of the house of Medici, no fear now of excommunication or dread of Interdict to Florentines for loyalty to the Medicis.

The fearful tragedy through which they had passed drew the people more closely to Lorenzo. They swore to stand by him with life and property. And like his grandfather Cosmo, Lorenzo knew how to make himself the beloved of the people. Though he ruled as a prince, he assumed no title, and preserved a republican form of government and went among the citizens as one of them, taking part in their carnivals and other amusements. The children knew and loved him.

At the suggestion of the artist Donatello, Cosmo di Medici placed his collection of ancient art in a garden which was opened to the public; this was the germ of the famous art gardens of Lorenzo. To all artists he extended the privilege of studying the many noble specimens of antique art in the Medici gardens. In these gardens the young Michael Angelo began his artist life. His clay models attracted Lorenzo, and he encouraged the youth to try his hand on marble. Michael Angelo was pleased with the suggestion, and chose a mutilated mask representing a laughing faun as his first subject. Lorenzo, on seeing the completed work, congratulated the youthful artist on his success, but remarked, "You have given the old faun all his teeth, at his age it is presumable that he had lost some." When Lorenzo came again to visit the young artist, he noticed that the old faun had lost an upper tooth, and the gum was so drilled as to give the appearance of its having fallen out. The aptitude of the youth pleased Lorenzo so much that he not only took him under his special patronage, but offered him a home in his house and he treated him as a son.

Lorenzo di Medici was an accomplished scholar and writer, and a valuable friend to men of letters and to artists. By his example in private life, in public addresses, and through his writings, he brought the native tongue into general use and into such high respect, that it became the language of the state and of literature. He established schools in the city and in all parts of the republic of Florence; he also greatly enlarged and adorned the city of Florence, and he delighted to attract to her both genius and talent. Through his influence Savonarola was called to Florence, and it was equally through his influence that Savonarola was elected prior of the convent of San Marco, a favorite monastery with the di Medicis. Cosmo had it rebuilt on a grand scale, and Lorenzo bestowed upon it a valuable library.

Savonarola was called to Florence in the same year that Michael Angelo became an inmate of the Medici palace. Michael Angelo regarded Lorenzo with love and gratitude. Savonarola believed that his call to Florence, to the prior-ship of San Marco, was from God. "Lorenzo," he declared, "is but an instrument in His hand, to effect His will, and gratitude is not due to an instrument." Savonarola regarded Lorenzo as a worldly-minded man, whose chief pleasures were in worldly vanities, and he refused to hold intercourse with such a man.

From the time that Cosmo rebuilt the convent, it became the rule that each newly elected prior should acknowledge the honor—to the ruling di Medici—by calling at the palace of the di Medici. Savonarola positively refused to comply with the custom, neither would he allow the convent to continue to appropriate the liberal donations of Lorenzo,—he required that they should be turned over to institutions needing assistance, and to other charities. Lorenzo did not resent the rudeness of the prior, he paid no attention to what he regarded as fanatical language and conduct. He admired the talents, the courage of his convictions and the unselfishness of the man, and allowed him, unmolested, to govern the convent in his own way. And so the time passed peacefully and happily in Florence to the close of the brief life of Lorenzo the Magnificent.

When he lay on his death bed he sent for Savonarola,—he came, but refused to see the sick man. Count Pico, alike friend to the friar and to the ruler, expostulated with the friar upon his unchristian conduct, and succeeded in convincing him that he was not acting in accordance with the spirit of Christ. Savonarola then consented to go to the sick room and perform the service for the dying. Politian writes, "Lorenzo made the responses in a tone so firm and gentle that men might have thought the friends present, with trembling voices, were the dying ones, not Lorenzo." In the year 1492 A. D., a memorable year, Lorenzo di Medici departed this life, aged forty-four years, the most illustrious of the rulers of Florence. The whole city bewailed his death, and well they might, for the sun of her glory set with him.

From the time of his death to the fall of the republic Florence was in a continuous state of change and disorder; tumults and anarchy at times prevailed. During one of these fearful tumults, Michael Angelo escaped to Venice and, after a brief stay, went from there to Bologna. The growing reputation of the young artist induced the Duke of Bologna to attach him to his court, and as court artist Michael Angelo remained two years in Bologna, but the increasing jealousy of the native artists caused him to return to his native city, but he did not find it the same Florence he had left. In less than three years an entire change had been wrought. The palace of di Medici, once his delightful home, was an empty ruin, the famous gardens where he had studied were a scene of desolation; pictures and statuary had been destroyed, the old joyous life was gone; of his artist friends, many had fled. Those who remained had become disciples of Savonarola, and Savonarola had become the soul of Florence.

This remarkable man was born in Ferrara in 1452. His nature had an intense religious bent which manifested itself through all his childhood. He took no pleasure in the sports of boys, always looking on the solemn side of life his heart warmed only to the church. As a young man he privately left his father's house, went to Bologna and sought admission in a Dominican convent. His parents were anxious that he should study medicine and succeed his grandfather who was a distinguished physician. On leaving home Savonarola left a letter to his father stating the necessity laid upon him to pursue the course he was taking.

He was received in the convent, and for six years he remained a humble brother of his order, occasionally visiting other cities to give spiritual instruction and to hear confessions. But there was no sign of the smouldering fire of his eloquence until all unexpectedly at Brescia it burst forth with such power that it shook men's souls and drew them awe-struck to the foot of the altar. His lips seemed touched with the live coal of prophecy; he foretold the terrible doom impending over Italy, especially over Brescia.

The prophetic fire continued to burn in his soul,

and he, with an impassioned eloquence which made men tremble before him, declared the judgments of the Lord against the country on account of the general wickedness, and more especially the wickedness of those who had been called to minister in holy things. He summoned the clergy and all Italy to humble themselves in deep repentance before the Lord that His hand might be stayed in the outpouring of the vials of His wrath. Savonarola's fame as a preacher was established before his call to Florence.

His power over the minds of men was remarkable; he seemed to hold the souls of his hearers in his hand, and his influence continued to increase until it bore him to the grand climax, legislator and ruler of Florence, but still continuing to be the great preacher. Multitudes thronged to hear him. The church of San Marco was too small, he must go to the great cathedral, and it became so crowded that men climbed the walls to catch, through the windows, a glimpse of his keen, delicate features and to hear his deep, thrilling voice.

CHAPTER XXXII.

SAVONAROLA.

IN the deplorable condition to which the rivalry of factions and the general disorder had reduced Florence, the signory and citizens called Savonarola from his convent—where his government was considered a model government—to come to the rescue of the city, to frame a government and to restore order. Savonarola obeyed the call; he summoned the men of the city to meet him in the cathedral; the summons was promptly obeyed and Savonarola submitted to the assembly four great principles on which to found their constitution: "Fear God; Prefer the good of the State before personal advantage; Grant a general amnesty; Form a great council,—have no parliament." The great council was to be composed of men of blameless character, over thirty years of age, whose fathers had served in former governments.

Among the many orders of magistrates which he instituted, was one of young men and youths, who were to ferret out blasphemers and gamblers and cite them before the great council; they were to seize all cards and dice, and they were to admonish all women and young girls who wore costly attire. This young order of magistrates not only fulfilled their orders, but were zealous to exceed them; they forced themselves into houses and took out mirrors, masks, perfumes, music and books of classic poetry. Savonarola commended them for their religious zeal, and this from him was to them an honor superior to that of knighthood, for he was both temporal and spiritual prince of Florence, although without the title. To gratify the native love of public spectacular exhibitions, he organized "The Procession," which at the same time gave a religious object lesson. A tabernacle was carried to the public square and men clad in white marched before it, singing and chanting as they went; they were followed by thousands of children, all clad in white and joining in the song. As they passed San Marco's, a red cross was given to each one in the procession. The procession stopped at the church of Santa Maria dei Fiore; on the altars of the church were vases for offerings, into which were poured gold and jewels, beside the altars were chests for costly hangings and gorgeous robes.

The next year, 1497, Savonarola desired to make "The Procession" still more impressive by being what he considered more intensely religious. "Florence should make a more costly sacrifice of her vanities and worldly treasures; the people should be compelled to surrender whatever offended monkish austerity. Florence was stripped of all that was elegant and beautiful."

It is estimated that twenty thousand crowns would not cover the cost of the valuable articles which were arranged in a pile to be burned, a spectacle to delight fanatics.

The pope was offended at the proceedings of the friar on the previous year, and had appointed a commission of Dominican theologians to deliberate upon the teachings and the conduct of Savonarola, and that commission, with one exception, had condemned him as guilty of heresy and of disobedience. But the pope was averse to extreme proceedings against Savonarola and sought to silence him by the offer of an archbishopric. The offer was of no avail, Savonarola was supreme ruler of Florence and the pulpit was his throne, and with fiery eloquence he hurled denunciations against pope, kings and people. He spared none whose works were wicked.

Savonarola's imagination was neither brilliant nor far-reaching, yet he forced home-truths upon his hearers in such an impassioned manner and in such burning words that they were often wrought up to a state of frenzy, a condition of mind not calculated to bring forth lasting good.

After "The Procession" of 1497 the pope determined to delay no longer. Savonarola was interdicted from preaching and the pope hurled against him a bull of excommunication for heresy. Savonarola protested against the charge of heresy, and appealed to his sermons and to his book, "The Triumph of the Cross," in proof of the correctness of his protest.

Shortly after, Florence was stricken with the plague, and during that sad time papal bulls were forgotten.

Savonarola would not leave the plague-stricken city, though pleasant places of retirement were urged upon him. When the city had partially recovered from the terrible pestilence, the friends of Savonarola besought the pope to withdraw the sentence of excommunication, and he would have withdrawn it but for being angered anew against the friar on account of the course he had pursued in crushing a late conspiracy against his government. The pope was so incensed that he issued a brief interdicting Savonarola not only from preaching in general but from preaching in San Marco's. Savonarola obeyed the letter of the brief but evaded the spirit by giving exhortations, or conferences, as his talks were termed, to sustain the faith and encourage the zeal of his followers. But the people of Florence after a time grew restive under the restriction, and during the winter they pressed Savonarola to preach again in public. He consented, and preached in the cathedral. It was crowded with eager listeners who by his contagious eloquence were borne along as by a flood. But notwithstanding the enthusiasm of the multitude, his austerities had created a faction in the city against him, and some of the most hostile excited a tumult around the cathedral and assailed the building with stones, but the Signory sustained him as a preacher as well a ruler.

Savonarola has been called "an incarnate idea, animated, urged and sustained by one purpose." He resolved that "The Procession" of 1498 should exceed the former processions in magnificence. Superb banners, sacred images, and other rich symbols were added, to gratify both spiritual pride and the love of display. For this procession the ferrets were to make their work exhaustive. No hidden garment of Babylon was to escape them, marble busts, pictures, all secular books, personal ornaments and elegant clothing were to be searched out and seized, to form a pyre for the burning. Deep indignation possessed those who were compelled to give up their treasures; the storm was brewing which eventually burst with such fearful force. Guards were stationed around the pyre to prevent the precious goods from being withdrawn or stolen. When the torch was applied and the flame of the burning treasure arose in the air, it was greeted with a burst of sacred song and the Te Deum was chanted to the sound of trumpets and the clanging of bells.

The news flew to Rome; not only the pope but the people of Rome were enraged. The pope threatened Florence with the Interdict. Savonarola again withdrew to San Marco, and from his pulpit hurled denunciation against the pope. He vowed that a wicked pope is no pope. Not content with that, he wrote to the great potentates, calling on them "to unite and depose a pope who is no pope, but a man who obtained the triple crown by fraud and perfidy, and is moreover an atheist." One of these letters was intercepted by the Duke of Milan, who sent it to the pope. He was furious in his rage, and issued a bull ordering the Signory to execute without delay the former decrees. The Signory appointed a commission of twelve men to act in the matter. The commission reported that for the public good, it was necessary that Savonarola should retire to San Marco and refrain altogether from preaching. For the peace of Florence, Savonarola consented to abide by the decision of the commission. The pope was content to have his great adversary silenced.

Savonarola might have lived peacefully in his convent to the end of his days but for the contentions of the Dominican and Franciscan monks. The Franciscans threw doubt and contempt on the prophetic inspiration, claimed for the Dominican prior of San Marco; the Dominicans resented this and asserted the claim more confidently; the Franciscans challenged proof by the ordeal of trial by fire. The Dominicans eagerly accepted the challenge. Two ardently devoted disciples of Savonarola, Buonvicini and Maruffi, besought the friar to permit one of them to act as his champion and pass through the fire in his stead. Each man was eager to be chosen. To content them the privilege was granted to both, and all things were put in order for the terrible ordeal, to which Buonvicini looked forward as to a triumph.

On the public square two huge piles of combustibles were erected, one hundred and twenty feet long, with a narrow pathway between them. On the Saturday before Palm Sunday, 1498, the piles were set on fire. A vast concourse of people assembled early in the morning eager to witness the spectacle, some questioning a favorable result, others claiming as certain the miraculous preservation of the men who represented the great friar. The Dominicans erected an altar on one side of the pile, the Franciscans on the other. In San Marco's, Savonarola celebrated mass. After the service the brethren formed in procession, preceded by Savonarola clad in his priestly robes, and bearing the Host. They moved in silence to the place of trial. On reaching the altar, as Savonarola placed the Host thereon, a burst of solemn song arose from the procession. During the chant Buonvicini knelt at the altar. The Franciscans kept silence, awaiting the signal to advance to the trial. The confidence of the Dominicans must have alarmed the Franciscans, for when the signal was given, instead of advancing they began to clamor about magic and the arts of enchantment. The concourse took up the cry, some for, some against, and a scene of general confusion ensued. Unperceived a storm had gathered, and in the height of the uproar it burst over the city, and the rain fell in torrents. When the storm abated, so that the voice of the Signory could be heard, they proclaimed that the sudden storm and drenching rain were the voice of God against the ordeal of trial by fire, and they dare not proceed in a trial against which God had manifested his displeasure. The crowd was ordered to disperse, and the Orders to retire to their convents.

The dispersing crowd hissed and scoffed Savonarola for permitting his friends to become his champions. The excitement rose to such a height against him that he and his friends had to be placed under the protection of a military guard. The next day San Marco's was assailed by an infuriated mob, which forced its way into the convent, though the monks made a desperate resistance. In the midst of the fight an order was brought by the guards from the Signory for the arrest of Savonarola, Buonvicini and Maruffi. The three men were brought out as bound prisoners. Still they would have been torn to pieces by the mob, but for the crossed halberds of the guards.

When the pope learned what had transpired he ordered that Savonarola should be conveyed forthwith to Rome, but the newly elected Signory, hostile to Savonarola, insisted that Florence had the right to try the prisoner. The change in the sentiment of Florence pleased the pope. He allowed the claim, and commended the Signory and people of Florence as true and faithful children of the Holy See.

The prisoners were not permitted any intercourse, not even the satisfaction of seeing one another. Their judges were chosen from among their enemies and their examination was by torture. But the extremity of torture could not induce Buonvicini to recant or to utter a word against his master. Maruffi was overpowered with terror at the sight of the rack, under the terrible agony of the torture his spirit failed, he recanted, he acknowledged any charge brought against himself or his master. The intrepid spirit of Savonarola failed under the torture of the rack, but when released from the horrible torture he withdrew his recantation and bewailed the weakness of the flesh. In the quiet of his cell, so long as writing materials were allowed him, he restated his doctrine in writing and continued his commentary on the psalms.

When his death sentence was pronounced he heard it in calm silence, but begged to be permitted to see his two brethren before being taken back to his cell. The request was granted, the guard conducted him to the cell of Buonvicini, who rejoiced to again behold and to grasp the hand of his beloved master with whom on the morrow, through the terrible gate of fire he would pass into the spirit world. On reaching the cell of Maruffi he found him in an agony of grief at the prospect of the fearful suffering, but the poor man grew calm in the presence of his fellow sufferer and father in the gospel. As he had done with Buonvicini so with Maruffi Savonarola prayed fervently and gave him his blessing. It was past midnight when he was led back to his cell. A friendly monk remained at his side during those last hours of his life; Savonarola laid his head on the lap of his friend and slept quietly till the morning.

The place for the execution was the same that had been used for the trial by fire. A platform was raised and on it a huge triple cross was erected; at the foot of the cross faggots were heaped. When the prisoners were brought to the place of execution they were clad in sackcloth; on the platform priestly robes were put on them only to be roughly torn off, as a ceremony of degradation. When Savonarola's friar's frock was jerked from off him, the bishop of Vassona spoke with a loud voice, saying, "I separate you from the church militant and from the church triumphant." Savonarola in a firm voice replied, "From the church militant, yes,—from the church triumphant, no; your power does not reach there."

Buonvicini and Maruffi were bound to the outer crosses, Savonarola was then secured to the central beam, the faggots were fired and the flame soon arose, but a sudden gust of wind blew the flames away from the bodies. Weeping friends exclaimed, "A miracle!" But the wind soon ceased, the devouring flames leaped up, and the mob yelled.

Before the sunset of that sad day the ashes of Savonarola and of his two friends had been gathered up and cast into the Arno.

Before that generation passed away Florence felt her shame and bewailed her loss, but, alas! too late.

CHAPTER XXXIII.

Characteristics of Savonarola.

UNDER some aspects Savonarola was a great reformer and harbinger of the reformation, but unlike Luther he would have held the world in sacerdotal bondage; he was essentially a monk, the "Incarnate Idea" would have striven to establish not only in Florence, but over Italy, yea, over the world, a sacerdotalism founded on uprightness of conduct and holiness of life, but essentially narrow and domineering.

Savonarola firmly believed in his divine mission as the prophet of the Lord and wrote "The Compendium Revelationum" to substantiate his claim to the prophetic office. In that work he teaches that "God reveals futurity to his chosen servants either by supernatural light infused into their souls, or by flashing knowledge of things to come directly upon their minds, or by visions, or through attending angels." Both mystic philosophers and mystic theologians apply the term *extatics* to a certain abstracted exaltation and illumination of mind from which proceed visions and revelations. Many instances may be cited, notably the Abbot Joachim, St. Theresa and Baron Swedenborg. Possibly persons who are enthusiastic and intensely religious may, through continuous concentration of feeling and of thought upon the unseen and mysterious, be borne into such an ideal region, that the ideal becomes so realistic that all doubt of the truth of their visions is removed, and along with this comes the consciousness of prophetic power. Or it may be that the mystics have crossed the border line of some one of the unexplored regions of human nature.

CHAPTER XXXIV.
THE ART KING.

THE great artist, Michael Angelo, was the descendant of an old Florentine family which claimed imperial blood and were people of note in Florence as early as 1250. When the artist returned from Bologna, he found that Florence was no longer a congenial home, but being an ardent patriot, he was full of indignation against the unworthy descendants of the great Lorenzo, for attempting to subvert that form of government which had been supported and administered by their illustrious forefathers.

The government of Savonarola, though nominally a republic, was more nearly allied to autocracy than to democracy, and it meant destruction to his beloved art. Had Michael Angelo remained in Florence, sooner or later there must have been collision between the two men; for the artist would have claimed the right to have classical as well as scriptural subjects, notwithstanding Savonarola's efforts to purge the city of heathen art.

Michael Angelo, in the privacy of his studio, executed a sleeping Cupid, but in the disturbed condition of the city he could neither exhibit, nor sell it. A relation of the great Lorenzo's advised Michael Angelo to give the marble an antique look, promising to see that the statue should be conveyed safely out of the city.

The artist gave to the marble a weather-worn appearance, and true to his promise di Medici sent the statue to Rome on consignment to his agent there. When the statue was placed on exhibition it excited great admiration, and by judges of art was regarded as a genuine antique. An art-loving cardinal bought it at a high price. The agent returned less than a fourth of the amount received to the artist in Florence. But rumors soon began to circulate in Rome that the cardinal's costly antique was in truth a modern work from Florence. The cardinal did not believe the rumor, but determined to investigate the matter, and sent a gentleman of his household to Florence, ostensibly in search of a sculptor competent to undertake an important work in Rome. On reaching Florence, the gentleman made known the wish of the cardinal and requested a general attendance of the artists of Florence at his apartments with specimens of their work. The artists were not slow to respond, taking with them specimens of their work. The young Angelo, but twenty-two years old, brought no specimen of his work; but when his time came, he took a pen and with a few bold lines drew a perfect human hand. The gentleman looked on in amazement at the readiness and excellence of the work, and begged to know what works the young artist had completed. Michael Angelo enumerated his finished works, including the sleeping Cupid. The gentleman was so impressed with the young artist that he requested him to remain. When alone the gentleman disclosed the true purpose of his visit, and told the young artist that all Rome had regarded his Cupid as a genuine antique, and that for the exquisite statue the cardinal had paid a very high price. Michael Angelo's indignation was at once aroused against the dishonest agent, and he resolved to go immediately to Rome and take measures to compel the man to pay him what he owed him. The gentleman urged him to go and to remain. "Rome," he said, "not Florence, is the place for such as you." The gentleman also pressed him to make his home with him.

In the summer of 1496 Michael Angelo removed to Rome, and worked with tireless industry, step by step gaining the peerless height which he eventually reached.

When his Pieta—Mary, mourning over the dead Christ, whose head rests on her lap—was exhibited, the beholders were so impressed with the work that by universal consent the artist was called Michael Angelo the Divine. Of this group, Grimm says:—
"The oftener it is contemplated the more touching does its beauty become, the purest nature, the noblest elements of the national Jewish expression and the unusual finish are linked with the wonderful harmony of the whole. Whatever previous to this work had been produced in Italy passes into shadow for something was lacking either in idea or execution; in this group both are completed and the result deserves to be called perfect." After completing this great work, Michael Angelo, on account of family matters, returned to Florence, and during his stay in that city he executed the group now known as the Madonna of Bruges, a life sized statue of Mary. She is seated, and enveloped in the softest drapery; the child Jesus is standing between her knees. This group ranks among his finest works, and during this visit to Florence he executed his famous statue of David; on this great statue he worked so diligently that he completed it in less than three years; and then the difficulty was, where should the great statue be placed? It weighed 18,000 pounds.

After the Signory had decided that it should stand on one of the pillars of the gate of the palace of government, the difficulty was how to get it there. The difficulty was at last overcome by building around the statue a wooden framework or open room, in which the statue was placed in an upright, swinging position by means of strong ropes passing under the huge limbs of the youthful giant, the ends of the rope were secured to the upper beams of the room or huge cage. The entire side of the artist's workshop had to be taken down to get the great cage out. It was placed on fourteen oiled beams and these were drawn slowly along by means of pulleys. Four days were occupied in drawing it to its destination. The elevation of the statue was a matter of such anxious and general concern that it formed an epoch in the history of the city; for a long time the people made their reckoning from it.

On his lofty pedestal David still stands in the majesty of youthful beauty, in his right hand he holds the sling, his left hand is raised as though about to put a stone in it. From the day of his elevation to the present day, the people of Florence regard the young David as their *genius loci*.

Michael Angelo's works in marble were numerous and all were great, but his crowning glory is his Moses, executed for the mausoleum of Pope Julius II. For forty years he worked on that superb statue, but in the meantime he executed groups and statues in marble and in bronze. All critics are agreed that his Moses is unsurpassed in ancient or in modern art. Michael Angelo's Moses is not a meek Moses, it is a grand, self-conscious Moses, conscious of the responsibility and of the power which God has entrusted to him, and conscious too, that he must gain self-mastery before he can be the leader and law-giver of his people.

Moses is seated but seems on the point of rising, the tables of the law are under his arm, his hand is in his beard which falls in heavy wavy locks on his breast. "The Moses is the crown of modern sculpture, not only in idea, but in the execution which is beyond comparison, and rises to a delicacy that could hardly be carried further." The force of character in the great law-giver is strikingly brought out in the expression of his countenance, and as a whole, the statue is a
"monument of art
Unparalleled,—language seems to start
From his prompt lips, and we his precepts own."

The chief paintings of Michael Angelo are in the Sistine Chapel at Rome, of these magnificent works the first is The Creation; God is here represented as an idealized, venerable man with a full flowing beard.

This superb figure is evidence of the belief of the artist that man is a personal as well as a spiritual image of Him who speaks in voice sublime and it is done. In the great painting God is brooding over the waters as He divides the light from the darkness, thereby calling day and night into being. The waters gather together in one place and the dry land appears, grass begins to put forth, then herbs and trees. The two great lights appear, the greater light to rule the day, the lesser light to rule the night. In the water moving creatures appear, and in the open firmament winged creatures fly. Jehovah is softly and slowly descending, angel hosts are thronging closely about Him, His mighty mantle is wide out-flowing, surrounding all the group. A drapery of violet-gray clouds falls closely around the divine form, through which the majestic beauty of that form may be clearly seen. Infinite power and almighty love beam from the sublime face.

On the summit of a dark mountain which the Creator is nearing, lies the beautiful body of Adam. God reaches out His right hand, and as though the divine motion conveyed a faint thrill of life, Adam raises his left hand and almost touches the finger of God, who takes the uplifted hand and at once the prostrate body is quickened into life. With the most natural movement, Adam arises and stands on his feet. Then comes the bestowal of life upon Eve. Adam lies sleeping on his right side, Eve is standing back of him, slightly bending forward, her arms are raised and her hands clasped in prayer; in this great picture prayer is her first expression of life. Then follow in historic order, the temptation, the fall and the expulsion from Eden. The scene of the temptation is full of deep thought; the conception is very different from that of Milton and much more profound.

This wonderful picture of the *Creation* follows the course of Bible history on to the time of the prophet

Jonah, and intermingled with Biblical scenes are figures from classic mythology; but whether from Biblical or mythical sources, every delineation bespeaks the rare combination of poet and artist in Michael Angelo.

The great picture was painted in the early prime of the artist's manhood. Thirty years afterward, on the side walls of the same chapel, he painted "*The Last Judgment*," on which he worked eight years without aid. During the progress of the work the master of ceremonies to the pope complained to his holiness of the many nude figures in the painting, declaring that it was improper to have such a crowd of naked people on the walls of the pope's chapel. The pope laughed at the man's prudery, but he submitted the complaint to the artist, whereupon Michael Angelo painted in the portrait of the man with the ears of an ass, and made him master of ceremonies to Satan. This great painting was completed near the close of the year 1541. It represents Christ with triumphant majesty in his countenance, seated on the throne of judgment. Around him are circles of angels, the circle nearest to him are calmly waiting in happy expectancy to hear their welcome sentence: Well done, good and faithful servants. The outer circle is excited, and that excitement spreads on all sides to the outer throng which is pressing toward the Judge, whose hands are upraised—eternal happiness on his right hand—eternal misery on his left.

An eminent historian says: "For the Roman nations Dante built up a new heaven and earth by remodeling the forms of pagan antiquity for his Christian mythology, and by endowing with tangible life what before existed in intangible mysticism; but Dante's great work lived only in the imagination until Michael Angelo embodied it in life-like forms."

When the great artist was in his seventieth year he was called to exercise his wonderful genius and skill in a comparatively fresh field of art. The pope appointed him architect and director of the building of the new St. Peter's. Michael Angelo was unwilling to accept the appointment, but at the entreaty of the pope he consented to undertake the work, and he set about it with his usual energy.

Under Julius III. a faction was raised against the artist on account of his rejection of inferior materials. This caused quite a heavy loss to those who supplied them, and these men won over some of the leading cardinals to their side. They succeeded the more readily, because the cardinals in charge of St. Peter's were piqued against Michael Angelo for not consulting them in reference to the changes he made in the remodeling the church. It was to them no small gratification to lay a complaint against him before the pope. The charges they brought were that Michael Angelo expended large sums of money without consulting them; that he did not communicate to them the manner in which the building was to be carried on; that he paid them no more consideration than if they had been ordinary and useless men. To satisfy the complaining cardinals the pope called a council, and caused Michael Angelo to be summoned to appear before the council to answer to the charges laid against him. The council met. The pope was present and so was the artist. The cardinals laid before the pope the further complaint that the interior of the church was made too dark by Michael Angelo's arrangement of the transverse arches. The artist was called to answer to this serious charge. He arose, saying: "I intend, your Holiness, to place three other windows above those already there." "You did not inform us of your purpose," replied the complainants. "I was not aware that I was under an obligation to do so," answered the artist, and continued, "and, moreover, I will not bind myself to give to your lordships, nor to anyone else, information of my intentions. Your office is to furnish money, and to see that it is not wasted. The plan of the building concerns me alone." Turning to the pope he said: "Your Holiness knows that I am not doing this work for money; that I have constantly refused payment; that I am doing the work for the good of my soul. If it does not tend to that, I have expended time and labor in vain."

"Have no fear of that," answer the pope, laying his hand on the artist's shoulder. The complaint was dismissed, and during the pope's life no man dared to make further complaint against Michael Angelo.

Under Pope Pius IV. complaints were laid against the artist of pulling down more than he put up. When Michael Angelo heard of the complaints, he applied to the pope for dismissal from the post of chief architect of St. Peter's. He said to the pope: "Your Holiness knows that I have worked seventeen years without compensation, and what I have done during that time is evident to all; and permit me to assure you that the dismissal I ask will be a welcome release." The pope would not grant the dismissal, on the contrary, he issued a Brief decreeing that the plans of Michael Angelo in the future were not to be departed from in any particular. The untiring industry of Michael Angelo for the succeeding three years strikes the student of biography with astonishment,—a man nearing ninety years working with a constancy and energy that would be remarkable for a man of forty-five.

Though in the main St. Peter's is built after the design of Michael Angelo, the church is not a full expression of his design, his plan was in part frustrated by the changes made after his death. Only the mighty dome is a complete expression of his matchless genius.

In the latter part of the year 1563, failing strength compelled him to rest from work, and in February, 1564, Michael Angelo departed this life, aged ninety years.

Michael Angelo, the sculptor, the architect, the poet, and the painter, was the man in whom modern art reached its highest expression; and he was the man whose integrity, industry, frugality and generosity proved that he had learned the great lesson that "*life* is the finest of the fine arts."

Michael Angelo was of a rather melancholy temperament; he loved solitude and simplicity. The brightest, the most cheerful part of his life were the five years of friendly intercourse with the gifted and sweet-natured Victoria Colonna.

After the funeral obsequies in Rome were over his friends, fearing that Rome would claim the right of his interment, concealed the coffin containing his remains in a load of merchandise to be delivered in Florence; the remains were in his native city before it was known in Rome that they had passed out of the gates of that city. On the arrival of the honored remains in Florence they were at once taken to the church of San Piero-Maggiore; a gold bordered pall of black velvet was placed over the coffin and a golden crucifix on it. The artists gathered in a close circle around the coffin, which was to be removed to the church of San Croce for interment. Under a star-lit sky the procession passed out from San Piero; the elder artists, with lighted torches, led the way; the younger artists bore the coffin; as they passed into the street a multitude of people joined in the procession. On reaching the church of San Croce, the coffin was opened; silently the multitude filed into the church to gaze, for the last time, on the face of Michael Angelo. Though he had been dead more than two weeks there was not a symptom of bodily decay; his face was unchanged, looking just as it did when the spirit took its flight. Funeral orations and funeral honors continued to be paid to his memory for many months.

In the same church in which Michael Angelo was buried are the remains of Dante and of Machiavelli. In the church of San Croce still stand the monuments of these three most gifted sons of Florence.

CHAPTER XXXV.

THE FATHER OF MODERN HISTORY.

LIKE Dante, Machiavelli was exiled in life and honored in death.
Like Michael Angelo, Machiavelli was an ardent patriot. His childhood was spent amidst the struggles and tumults with which the factions of the nobles filled Florence. He was ten years old when the conspiracy of the Pazzi was crushed, and with the enthusiasm of boyhood he embraced the cause of the great citizen, Lorenzo. He grew to manhood under the happy administration of the great Lorenzo, but while yet a young man the death of Lorenzo left the republic exposed to internal jealousies and to foreign ambition. He seems not to have taken part in the disturbances of the times, but to have quietly pursued his course as secretary to one of the chief officers in the court of chancery.

That he did not affiliate with the party of Savonarola is evident from an extant letter of his on Savonarola, whom he designates as "a man of daring assurance." By quiet gradations Machiavelli rose to the management of foreign affairs and diplomatic negotiations which he conducted for fourteen years or until the government was overthrown by the Medicean party. His superior power in diplomacy caused him to be frequently employed by the new government on important diplomatic missions, the satisfactory result of these missions won for him the confidence and favor of the government to such an extent that he was scarcely ever at home; on returning from one mission he was directed to prepare for another. His active diplomatic life continued up to the time when the government was overthrown by the help of Spanish arms.

The newly established government deposed Machiavelli. His indignation was aroused, and with burning eloquence he denounced the encroachments of the nobles. Nor yet did he spare the time serving Signory; they had to smart under his sharp rebukes and keen sarcasms. By a coalition between the signory and the nobles they secured his arrest and imprisonment as a disturber of the peace. While in prison, upon suspicion of his having knowledge of a newly discovered conspiracy against the government, he was put to the torture to compel him to confess what he knew of the plot and of those implicated in it. Under the terrible agony of the rack he preserved a patient endurance and an unshaken fortitude; he continued to affirm he had nothing to confess and no accusation against others could be wrenched from his lips. After a long imprisonment in a loathsome dungeon he was liberated on the testimony of many witnesses to his entire innocence of any complicity with the conspirators. On being liberated he was banished from Florence. Banishment from Florence from his public life was a hard fate to Machiavelli, but his complaints of the cruelty and injustice of the treatment he received availed him nothing.

In his banishment he sought to soothe the bitterness of his soul, not by dissipation, but by manual labor; he gave his mornings to actual hard work on the grounds of his country home. Soothed and calmed by laboring with his hands he would go indoors, refresh himself in the bath, put on his best clothes and go into his library, or as he expressed it, " enter the august assembly of great minds among whom I spent my best hours." During his banishment he wrote "The Prince," a work embodying the result of his observations upon the governments of his own time and of his study of the political principles of the ancients. The book was not published until after his death; it was then published in Rome under the sanction of Pope Clement VIII. Immediately it had an immense circulation, it was translated into nearly all the languages of Europe, even into Turkish, and it soon aroused a general howl of indignation because of its open advocacy of duplicity in the theory of government. According to "The Prince" force and fraud are justifiable when they can be made a means of securing political advantage or national safety.

The theory of government propounded in "The Prince" caused the name of Machiavelli to become a synonym for perfidious dealing. In the "Merry Wives of Windsor," the host of the Garter Inn asks, "Am I politic? Am I subtle? Am I a Machiavel?" But, taking the man in connection with his time, it seems an injustice to his memory. The leniency he advocates toward conquered people shows a different, a human side of his nature.

Pope Leo X. encouraged the solitary man by his kindly regard and appreciation; the pope requested him to prepare a plan for the remodeling of the government of Florence, and he employed him on a public mission, thereby raising Machiavelli's hopes that an active public career was again opening before him. But his pleasant anticipations, his cherished hopes, were soon destroyed by the death of the pope, for whom he grieved deeply. Subsequently his grief was turned into joy by the longed-for information that his name was again enrolled among the citizens of Florence, that he was again eligible to office. He returned to Florence happy in the belief that he should re-enter public life under favorable auspices. But he was doomed to disappointment, public feeling was against him, he was in the employ of the di Medici, who had again been expelled from the city.

Before the return of Machiavelli to Florence, Cardinal Julius commissioned him to write "The History of Florence;" when that admirable work was completed and presented, the Cardinal Julius had become Pope Clement VII. The pope was greatly pleased with the manner in which his commission had been executed.

THE FATHER OF MODERN HISTORY. 211

Of Machiavelli's History of Florence, Dr. Hallam says: "This great work is enough to immortalize the name of Machiavelli. Seldom has a more giant stride been made in any department of literature than by this judicious, clear and elegant history; preceding historical works, whether in Italy or out of it, had no claim to the praise of elegant compositions, whilst this history ranks among the greatest of that order. Machiavelli was the first who gave at once a luminous development of great events and their causes and connections. His view of the formation of European societies, both civil and ecclesiastical, on the ruins of the Roman Empire, had never been attempted before, though it may now seem to contain only what is familiar."

The nature of Machiavelli, as manifested both in his life and his writings, suggest the notion of a live bundle of co-working antagonistic elements. He is generous and he is selfish; he is benevolent and he is cruel; he is a profound philosopher and he is a comic wit; he has the grave impartiality of the historian and the one-sided keenness of the satirist; he has the warmth of poetic feeling, and the cold, shrewd sagacity of the diplomatist.

The man was the product of his times, and to understand him it is necessary to study the records of those times. But of the good influence of his writings on his native language there can be no question. It is similar to the influence of Addison on the English language. Machiavelli lived to see the last fatal struggle of Florence for liberty. The successful beginning of the struggle fired his patriotism, and with an impassioned love of country, he takes up the words of Petrarch:

> "Lo! valor against rage
> Shall take up arms, and in the fight,
>   Regain her ancient heritage.
> For patriot blood still warms Italian veins,
> Though low the fire, a spark at least remains."

Alas! the fire was so low that the commander-in-chief of the Florentine forces became a traitor to his country. Through him and his fellows in treachery Florence was vanquished by her ingrate sons. But had there been no traitors within her walls, had she come off victorious in her struggle, as at first seemed almost certain, it is scarcely probable that her freedom would have continued through even one lifetime, for the cancer of discord had so nearly eaten away her life, that there was not left enough of public spirit to maintain her liberty had it been achieved.

A republic must be an impartial mother, her children must all fare alike, have equal civil rights and privileges, if she is to have length of days and continue to be a power in the world. A republic with privileged classes of hereditary nobility is as a fair apple with a destroying worm at the core. The weakness of the Republic of Florence lay in idleness, dissipation and the lack of civil equality among her people, one class on every possible occasion desiring, striving, to override all others because of the titled distinction which they inherited.

The strength, the true glory of a Republic lies in the uprightness, the intelligence, the enterprise, and the industry of her people. In the continuous, Christian development of the dignity and greatness of human nature, as the centuries roll onward, developing out of the Past into the Future.

Thus may the human family advance until they grow into one world-wide Republic, emancipated from war, intemperance, and all kindred evils; and attaining a further penetration into the secrets of nature which are the wonders of science, through purity of life, industry and patient seeking. And further, attaining just conceptions of the Bible religion pure and undefiled, and a sacred sociality in "the roomy future, immense and palatial."

www.ingramcontent.com/pod-product-compliance
Lightning Source LLC
Chambersburg PA
CBHW020858230426
43666CB00008B/1234